MUHAMMAD IBN AHMED IBN IYAS

AN ACCOUNT OF THE OTTOMAN CONQUEST OF EGYPT IN THE YEAR 922 A.H (1516 A.D)

Translated from the third volume of the Arabic chronicle of Muhammed Ibn Ahmed Ibn Iyas, An eye-witness of the scenes he describes

Translated By - W. H. Salmon

Qadeem Press

Qadeem Press

Qadeem Press Edition
Breathing Life into Forgotten Pages
www.qadeempress.com

Originally Published by the Royal Asiatic Society in 1921
Reprinted by Qadeem Press in 2025

Find our titles on your favourite online bookstore using the keyword 'Qadeem Press'

FOREWORD

This translation was undertaken at the suggestion of Professor Margoliouth, and was almost completed when the outbreak of the Great War consigned the MS. to a drawer for five years.

Strangely enough, this War, which seemed to have obliterated all other war-stories, has brought the places mentioned by Ibn Iyās into fresh prominence; Damascus, Hamāh, Aleppo, and Homs, with Gaza and the routes from Syria to Egypt, have become familiar to us in our daily papers.

The barbaric splendours and appalling cruelties in the narrative seem to belong to remote times; as a matter of fact, it was the age of Henry VIII and François I, of Charles V and Luther, but the conquering Turk took no account of the Renaissance or the Reformation. Even at the present time the bulk of the nation seems to remain much as it was four centuries ago.

My best thanks are due to Professor Margoliouth, of Oxford, and to Mr. C. A. Storey of the India Office for the kind help they have given me in the solution of many difficulties.

W. H. Salmon.

57 Holland Park,
London, W.11.
1921.

INTRODUCTION

DURING the years which have elapsed since the translator of the following pages undertook his task the countries which the Sultan Selim I in his Eastern campaigns annexed to the Ottoman Empire have through the fortune of war been withdrawn from it, and Egypt, after four centuries of dependence, has again become the seat of a Sultanate. These extraordinary events, which were not anticipated when the work was begun, lend a special interest to a detailed and contemporary account of the victory which brought Egypt with its dependencies under Ottoman rule.

The story was told by von Hammer in his *Geschichte des Osmanischen Reiches* [1] mainly after Turkish and European authorities, and by G. Weil, in his *Geschichte der Chalifen*,[2] after Ibn Iyās and another contemporary Arabic account. Zinkeisen in his admirable Ottoman history followed von Hammer, and Sir W. Muir, in his *Mameluke or Slave Dynasty of Egypt*, was dependent on Weil. The very brief account in the latest Ottoman history on a large scale [3] rests apparently on the statements of European witnesses.

The work of Ibn Iyās which Weil used in MS. was published in three volumes at the Government Press, Boulaḳ, A.H. 1311–1312 1893–1895). It is called *Bada'i' al-zuhūr fī waqā'i' al-duhūr*, and is one of four works by the same author, all of which are preserved.[4] No biography of its author appears to have been discovered, but a little can be gleaned from his writings about his family and his career.[5] He informs us that he was born on Saturday 6 Rabī'ii, 852 (June 8, 1448),[6] so

[1] Vol. ii, book xxiv, Pest, 1828.

[2] Vol. v, chs. xxi, xxii, Stuttgart, 1862.

[3] N. Jorga, *Geschichte des Osmanischen Reiches*, ii, pp. 336–41, Gotha, 1909.

[4] Wüstenfeld, *Geschichtschreiber*, No. 513; Brockelmann, ii, 295; Vollers in *Revue d'Égypte*, 1895, pp. 544–73.

[5] See especially Vollers, l.c.

[6] ii, 144.

that in 922, when the events recorded in the extract took place, he was seventy (lunar) years old. His great-grandfather, the Amīr Izdomir 'Umarī Nāṣirī, known as the Khāzindār, after having been Amīr Silāḥ, was made by the Sultan Sha'bān viceroy of Tripoli.[1] Presently he was transferred to Ḥalab, and in 768 recalled and again made Amīr Silāḥ.[2] He was imprisoned for a time during an émeute in Cairo, but was released and appointed governor of Damascus, but died before he could start in 771.[3] This person had originally been a slave, and sold by the same merchant as the Amīr Shaikho, whom he succeeded as Amīr Silāḥ in 757. Of his *nisbahs* Nāṣirī is likely to refer to the Sultan of that name, and Saifī to his son the Sultan Saif al-dīn; he was then a Circassian slave, purchased by the first of these sovereigns and manumitted by the second. Ibn Iyās appears to say nothing of his father or grandfather, but mentions that his sister was married to one Ḳurḳmās, an Amir Ākhūr of the fourth class, who was called 'Alā'ī, and died in battle in the year 877.[3] He names among his shaikhs the famous polygraph, Jalāl al-dīn Suyūṭī, for whom he appears to have felt no great respect,[4] and 'Abd al-Bāsiṭ b. Khalīl the Ḥanefite, whose history (preserved in MS.) he cites.[5] He himself belonged to the same legal school, and had the honourable title Zain al-dīn or Shihāb al-dīn.

The Chronicle terminates at the end of 928, and its composition seems to have occupied a number of years. Thus a passage in II, 109, where it is stated that Aḥmad b. Abī Sa'īd is still on the Timurid throne, must have been written not later than 899, when the reign of that prince terminated,[6] and one of the existing MSS. bears a colophon, wherein the author asserts that the volume was finished on 15 Muḥarram

[1] i, 213, A.H. 764. For the titles in the text see Van Berchem, *Matériaux pour un Corpus Inscriptionum*, p. 451.

[2] ii, 221.

[3] ii, 144.

[4] ii, 119, 271, 307, 339, 392.

[5] ii, 104, 105; Wüstenfeld, l.c., No. 508.

[6] Vollers seems to have overlooked this.

915 (May 5, 1509).[1] This volume ends with the events of 912. For the period for which he is a contemporary authority, his work consists in the main of a court circular, recording the doings of the sovereign and the decorations which he confers; in this it resembles some of the chronicles of the Moghul Emperors. Into this framework various memorabilia are introduced, chiefly obituaries of distinguished men, but also public calamities, the movements of the market, and *causes célèbres*; to this last category belongs the discussion of the orthodoxy of the poet Ibn al-Fāriḍ, which occupies much space. At times contemporary verses, serious or satirical, are inserted. The composition of the court-circular must have been the business of some official, as also the preservation of the notices; it is possible that Ibn Iyās himself was employed by the government to discharge these duties, and this is rendered likely by the fact that he frequently cites his own poems, some of them encomia on men in power, which are likely to have been composed in some official capacity.

There is one feature about his history which counts as a defect with Oriental critics,[2] but as a merit among Western scholars; it is that it is written in a language which embodies much of the vernacular of the time, and in consequence is of value for the history of the Arabic language and the development of the Cairene dialect. Some of the expressions into which the author drops are still characteristic of the patois of Cairo; many phrases not as yet registered in any dictionary appear to be characteristic of the time. Some help for the understanding of such of them as are political technicalities is afforded by the two works on the Mamlūk state which have been published, but these leave much unexplained.

The suddenness wherewith the great Egyptian Sultanate collapsed before the Ottoman arms is the most impressive feature in the following narrative, and the explanation of it

[1] Weil, l.c., V, vi.
[2] See Gurgi Zaidān's *Ta'rikh Ādāb al-lughah al-'Arabiyyah*, iii, 298.

is perhaps to be found in the general course of Egyptian and Ottoman history rather than in the events which Ibn Iyās here records. The Mamlūk system produced a considerable number of eminent rulers, and, indeed, the mode of appointment was one calculated to bring talented men to the front. Still their rule was foreign military occupation, which was backed by no popular enthusiasm or loyalty. Ability to speak the Arabic language appears to have been exceptional in the case of these Sultans, whence the substitution of an Ottoman Pasha only affected the bulk of the people in so far as Cairo became the capital of a province instead of the metropolis of an empire. In order to resist the Ottoman conqueror the Egyptian Sultanate required able officers and trustworthy troops. It so happened that it had neither.

The defeat of Marj Dābaḳ is ascribed to the ill-feeling between the two sets of Mamlūks, the Ḳarāniṣah and the Jilbān, of whom the Sultan was supposed to favour the latter. Such jealousies between army corps are familiar in Muslim history; but what was the character of these bodies? It would seem that the definition of the Ḳarānīṣ offered by Khalīl al-Ẓāhirī is of little use for this question;[1] he says: "The ḳarānīṣ troops are those who migrated at an early period, and are attached to the Holy Bureau, possessors of ample stipends, designed for commissions, equal to commanders of fives;[2] their number was originally 100, but in our time is smaller. They are called *Ouloughlar.*" Von Hammer[3] infers from the texts that they were the lowest class of mercenary; for the accession-money which they received was on a certain occasion 30 ducats, whereas the Jilbān received 50 and the Mamlūks 100. The name perhaps occurs first in the Chronicle of Tangri-Bardi,[4] where it is stated that in the year 802 the army divided into two parties, one

[1] *Zubdat Kashf al-Mamālik*, ed. Ravaisse, p. 115.

[2] This meant that each had a small court of five Mamlūks. See van Berchem, *Corpus Inscriptionum*, p. 543 n.

[3] l.c., ii, 470 n.

[4] Ed. Popper, vi, 15, 7.

siding with the Amīr Itmish Bajāsi, these being all the greatest Amīrs and the Ḳarānīṣ Mamlūks, another with the Amīr Yashbak, these being the Amīrs of the Khāṣṣikiyyah and the Mamlūks of the Aṭbāḳ. In Ibn Iyās's Chronicle it is assumed that the reader knows the sense of this name, and all that we can learn is that it is in antithesis to Jilbān. In 897, after a plague which had carried off great numbers, the Sultan Ḳaietbai gave every one of his army, whether Ḳarāniṣah or Jilbān, a horse that had belonged to one of the deceased.[1] In 865 the Sultan Aḥmad b. Īnāl on the occasion of a Bedouin raid despatched against them a force wherein he sent none of the Jilbān Mamlūks; this greatly offended the Ḳarāniṣah, and they harboured mischief in consequence.[2] Now the form Jilbān (for which *Ajlāb* is occasionally substituted)[3] appears to be connected with the verb *jalaba* in the sense of importing a slave from a foreign country, which is often used by Ibn Iyās in explaining the origin of a Mamlūk Sultan;[4] the subject of the verb being in such cases the dealer. The Jilbān are at times called the Jilbān of a particular Sultan;[5] whence it would seem that Khalīl is right in defining the Ḳarāniṣah as early immigrants, though he seems to be wrong for the period with which we are dealing in the matter of their numbers and distinction. The etymology of the word is far from clear; *ḳurnāz* in Turkish is a familiar word for "sly", "cunning", and might serve to describe "an old campaigner". The practice of differentiating between different classes of troops in the matter of accession-money is said to have been introduced by the Sultan Īnāl in 857,[6] who is charged by the historian with meanness in this innovation; it is strange that the veterans should receive less than the new arrivals. In any case we must reject von Hammer's division of the Egyptian army into Mamlūks, Jilbān, who were in the main Abyssinian slaves, and Ḳarāniṣah, the lowest class of mercenaries. According to

[1] ii, 277. [2] Ibid. 68, end. [3] Ibid. 77, l. 3.
[4] ii, 15, 24, 39; cf. *infra*, p. 64. [5] ii, 67. [6] ii, 41.

our authorities, the name Mamlūk was common to all; and if there was any superiority it lay with the Ḳarāniṣah. In the narrative of Ibn Iyās it is the Jilbān who are constantly rioting and giving trouble.

Of one other division of the army, mentioned in this extract, Ibn Iyās has given a definition. This is the *aulād al-nās*, whom he identifies with the *ḥalḳah*.[1] Some account of the *ḥalḳah* is given in the *Zubdat Kashf al-Mamālik*,[2] where their numbers are stated to have been originally 24,000, chiefly employed in garrison duty. It seems likely that their name *The children of the Men* signifies that they were descendants of Mamlūks; and the interest which Ibn Iyās displays in their welfare indicates that he was connected with such a family. He thanks God on one occasion that their fiefs were restored to them after they had been taken away.[3] The Sultans seems to have been frequently tempted to disband them; the Sultan Ḳaietbai adopted with them the plan by which Penelope meant to get rid of her suitors; a heavy bow with a corresponding arrow was brought and all who were unable to draw it were dismissed.[4]

The death of a Circassian sovereign was regularly followed by disorders, as there was no hereditary loyalty, and the provincial governors regarded such an event as an opportunity for the assumption of at least independence. The new Sultan had to meet the demand for accession-money, frequently from an empty treasury. Hence the death of the Sultan Ghūrī on the field after a defeat by the mighty Selīm was more fatal to the Mamlūk Empire than such a disaster would have been to the Ottomans or any other government which had a nation behind it.

For the topography of Cairo, to which there are many allusions in this extract, reference should be made to the admirable works of Casanova and Van Berchem, which leave little unexplained. The Commentary of the latter on his

[1] i, 295. [2] p. 116. [3] ii, 47. [4] ii, 101.

Corpus Inscriptionum explains with great skill and learning most of the technicalities of the Mamlūk court.[1] M. Blochet in the preface to his translation of Makrīzī[2] has drawn up a list of 134 works, mostly unpublished, which deal with the history of the Moslem Egypt and its dependencies; it is to be hoped that the Egyptian Government, which has rendered many valuable texts accessible, may arrange for the publication of many more of those histories of the Mamlūk period which now lie scattered in various libraries, public and private.

D. S. MARGOLIOUTH.

[1] Since writing the above the author has learned that M. Van Berchem passed away on March 21 of this year. He had no rival in his own field of research.

[2] *Histoire d'Égypte de Makrizi*, Paris, 1908.

TABLE OF COMPARATIVE DATES

A.H. 922	Muḥarrem	A.D. 1516	Tuesday, February 5.
,,	Ṣafar	,,	Thursday, March 6.
,,	Rebi' i	,,	Friday, April 4.
	,, ii	,,	Sunday, May 4.
,,	Jumādā i	,,	Monday, June 2.
,,	,, ii	,,	Wednesday, July 2.
,,	Rejeb		Thursday, July 31.
	Sha'bān	,,	Saturday, August 30.
,,	Ramaḍān	,,	Sunday, September 28.
,,	Shawwāl	,,	Tuesday, October 28.
,,	Dhu'l Ḳa'dah	,,	Wednesday, November 26.
,,	,, Ḥijjah		Friday, December 26.

THE OTTOMAN CONQUEST OF EGYPT

THEN commenced the year A.H. 922; the first day of the month Muḥarrem was a Monday. The Khalīfah at that time was the Amīr of the Faithful, al-Mutewekkil 'alā Allāh Muḥammed Ibn Amīr al-Mu'minīn al-Mustemsik B'illāh Ya'ḳūb—may his honour be extolled! The Sulṭan of Egypt was al-Malik al-Ashraf Abū Naṣr Ḳānṣūh al-Ghūrī[1]—may his victories be glorified.

* * * * *

News was received in A.H. 922 of hostilities between Shāh Ismā'īl al-Ṣūfī, ruler of the two 'Irāḳs, and Selīm Shāh Ibn 'Othmān, Sulṭān of Constantinople. The fighting had apparently been begun in 920 by Shāh Ismā'īl al-Ṣūfī's invading the territory of Selīm Shāh. When the news reached the Sulṭān of Egypt, al-Ghūrī, he deemed it necessary to send an expedition to Aleppo and to accompany it himself, with the intention of remaining there to watch the results of the war between Shāh Ismā'īl al-Ṣūfī[2] and Ibn 'Othmān, for he was of opinion that whichever of the two came off victorious would forthwith invade his Egyptian dominions.

[19] On Wednesday and Thursday, the 20th and 21st of the first spring month, the Sulṭān al-Ghūrī issued pay to the rest of the troops, and on Saturday, 23rd, the Sulṭān paid all the Ḳarāniṣah[3] and imported Memlooks, and announced to them in his private grounds that the expedition would leave on the 1st of the following month. This caused some confusion amongst the troops, and generally throughout Cairo. Horses and mules became scarce, the Memlooks took to raiding the mills, taking away their horses and mules and

[1] In accordance with the practice of many Orientalists, I have spelt the Memlook Sulṭān's name "Ḳanṣūh al-Ghūrī". It is, however, noteworthy that—as I have learnt since completing the translation—on the page of a contemporary Ḳo'rān written for the Sulṭān himself and reproduced on plate 83 of Moritz's *Arabic Palæography*, the name is clearly written "Ḳānṣauh al-Ghaurī".

[2] More commonly known as "The Ṣafawī", i.e. descended from Ṣafī al-Dīn.

[3] Vide *Zubdat Keshf al-Memālik* (Ravaisse), p. 115.

old jades, in consequence of which all the mills closed down. No bread or flour was obtainable in the markets, the people were famishing and much distressed, and offered up many prayers. The cloth markets also closed on account of the Memlooks. The artisans and tailors concealed themselves, and Cairo was given up to general confusion. Numbers of merchants hid themselves for fear of the Memlooks, and many slaves also, for fear of being compelled to go on the expedition. It might have been the Day of Judgment in Egypt—every man was exclaiming: "O Lord! save my soul!"

The troops blamed the Sulṭān for all this excitement. He did not act as other Sulṭāns had done when they went on expeditions, and in spite of it all there was nothing to justify this great fuss and commotion. News had not come that Ibn 'Othmān or his advanced troops had reached Aleppo, neither had he invaded the Sulṭān's territory. They also blamed the Sulṭān for inspecting and paying the whole of the troops in four days; for they were afraid that this would be reported in the dominions of Ibn 'Othmān and al-Ṣūfī, and that the troops would be deemed numerically insignificant in consequence. They complained that there was no army in Egypt, and that the covetousness of the enemy would be excited when they heard this. But this was not correct, and it all showed a bad state of affairs.

On the Saturday previously mentioned the Sulṭān sent the chief Amīrs their pay. He sent 5,000 dīnārs to Atābek Sūdūn al-'Ajemī, 4,000 each to Amīr Arkmās, Amīr Mejlis, Amīr Sūdūn al-Dawādārī, chief of the guards, and to Amīr Anas Bai, chief chamberlain; and 3,000 dīnārs to each of the [20] chief Amīrs not holding special appointments—but what was this compared to what al-Ashraf Ḳāit Bai used to send to the chief Amīrs when they went on expeditions against Ibn 'Othmān. To Atābek Ezbek alone he had sent 30,000 dīnārs, and to Amīr Temrāz, Amīr Silāḥ [1] 20,000 dīnārs, and to the Amīr Mejlis a similar sum; as well as 10,000 dīnārs

[1] "Le chef des officiers qui portaient les pièces de l'armure destinée au Sultan, et qui les lui présentaient lorsqu'il en avait besoin" (Dozy).

apiece to all the other chief Amīrs, which was considered extraordinarily unusual. Al-Ashraf Ḳāit Bai did this only in his last expedition against Ibn 'Othmān in the year A.H. 895. The total allowances of the Amīrs, exclusive of the troops, amounted to 100,000 dīnārs.

On the first day of the week, and the 24th day of the month, the Sulṭān came down and went out to his college at Sharabishīyīn, where he remained until the afternoon, and it was reported that he had inspected the storehouses of the Queen-mother, whose possessions were there, and he found that she had much property, including a large amount of gold and silver specie, precious stones, costly clothing, and other things.

On Monday, the 25th, the Sulṭān issued advances to the Amīrs of Ṭablkhānah,[1] and to the Amīrs of Tens, summoning each one separately, as if he had been paying wages. He gave to each Amīr of the former 500 dīnārs and to each of the latter 200 dīnārs; but did not make any allowance to the Khalīfah, which was a source of much inconvenience to the latter, who entreated some of the Amīrs to lend him sums of money on usury, and ran heavily into debt in consequence. The Khalīfah had never before accompanied the Sulṭān on an expedition to Syria without an allowance. His baggage and equipment on expeditions had usually been borne by the Sulṭān, who allowed him 500 dīnārs as wages for his followers; but this Sulṭān paid no attention to anything of this kind, and was stingy towards him in the matter of allowances, so that the Khalīfah was hardly dealt with.

The Sulṭān then inspected the Ḳarānisah Memlooks, the old men and invalids, detailing some of them to his Sharḳīeh

[1] "Des tambours qui, joints à des trompettes et à d'autres instruments, se faisaient entendre à plusieurs moments du jour à la porte des souverains et des personnages élevés en dignité. Plusieurs émirs jouissaient de cette prérogative, et pour cette raison, chacun d'eux prenait le titre de Amīr Ṭablkhānah. Ils avaient sous leur commandement quarante ou quatre-vingts cavaliers, et le mot en question a reçu le sens de grade d'émir de quarante hommes" (Dozy).

and Gharbīeh provinces and to Upper Egypt, and compelling them to go without allowances. They amounted to about 500 Memlooks.

On Tuesday, the 26th, the Sulṭān came down from the citadel and went to Raidāniyyeh, and showed the Farrāshes [sweepers] how to set up the royal tent during the expedition. He also arranged for the quarters of the Amīrs at Raidāniyyeh. On the same day the Sulṭān instructed his son, the Grand Master of the Horse, to make his preparations to start with him. At first the Sulṭān commanded him to await his arrival at Bāb al-Silsilah; then he countermanded this and commanded him to get his baggage ready for the expedition.

On Friday, the 29th, corresponding to the 6th of the Coptic month Beshans, the Sulṭān took off his woollen garments and changed into white linen clothing. This was the first Friday since the death of the Sulṭān's wife. He arranged a splendid feast in her honour, at which the Khalīfah, the four judges, a number of the chief Amīrs, and all the readers of the town and the preachers were present. There were many people present on that night at the Sulṭān's college at Sharābishīyīn.

On Saturday, the 1st of the month Rebī' al-Ākhir, the Sulṭān sat in the Maidān; the Khalīfah and the four judges came to offer congratulations on the new month, and then returned to their homes. The same day the Sulṭān appointed [21] the son of the late Mihtār Ḥasan, the Master of the Cellar (of whose death mention has been made), to his father's office. On the 2nd he distributed to the imported Memlooks sets of coloured silk horse clothing, helmets, shields, and sets of bridles, steel stirrups, weapons, etc., from the armoury. The Memlooks crowded round him and began helping themselves to the fine clothing, and were not satisfied with what the Sulṭān distributed; he failed to pacify them that day, and at that time they became extremely insolent.

A Wonder.—It was said that a woman gave birth to a boy with two heads, four arms, and four legs; the Sulṭān was amazed when he saw it. It was said that a similar portent had appeared in the time of the Imām 'Alī.

Amongst the favours of Providence to the Faithful was the cancelling of his order by the Sulṭān for the departure of the Arabs, whom he had allotted to the Sharḳīeh and Gharbīeh provinces and to Upper Egypt. As before mentioned the Sulṭān had decided to take with him on the expedition a body of Arab cavalry to move in front of the troops in war. So he summoned the Arab Sheikhs and the overseers and instructed them to provide 500 mounted men, or according to some 5,000.

They went all over the country imposing on each small village the maintenance of two horsemen at 100 dīnārs, and four on the larger villages at 200 dīnārs. When the Fellāḥīn of the districts heard of this they left their villages and their crops and fled, so some of the villages became desolate in this movement.

When the Amīrs heard of this they went to the Sulṭān and complained to him about this, and said: "We are setting out with you, and our villages are destroyed; whence shall we get food and give pay to our followers?" The Sulṭān was put to shame by them, and ordered these doings to be stopped. He issued imperial edicts to the overseers and Sheikhs of the Arabs cancelling previous orders, and telling them to return what had been taken from the Fellāḥīn. The imperial edicts reached the villages, and but for them the whole of Egypt would have been devastated and overtaken by famine. God be praised for this deliverance!

Among the events of this time was the exaction of money by the Sulṭān from the daughter of Amīr Khāir Bey, Inspector of the Gharbīeh Province. She was the wife of Amīr Tānī Bey, the treasurer and one of the chief Amīrs, and was the person implicated in the degrading affair before mentioned. When the Sulṭān made a claim against her for a large sum of money, he sent a number of eunuchs to demand this money. Upon which she set to work to sell her dowry and all her stock and other property. On the death of her father, Amīr Khāir Bey, some enemies had accused her of taking property of his, consisting of three jars containing a large sum of money. The Sulṭān sent for her, and on her coming into his presence questioned her about the matter. She denied it all, and swore that she had never even seen these jars of gold which they accused her of taking. The Sulṭān became angry with her, and said: "Have you forgotten your crime about the child which they found with you?" He swore that unless she produced her father's property which she had taken he would drown her, and he meant to do it. She then set about selling her dowry to pay the money demanded of her. On every [22] Saturday and Tuesday Zeinī Berekāt Ibn Mūsā and a number of officials used to come and sell her clothing, just as they would the effects of a deceased person.

An exactly similar thing had happened to the daughter of Yashbek the Dawādār, the wife of Amīr Ḳān Bai, Grand Master of the Horse; she had money exacted from her, and sold her dowry, her clothes, and her slaves like the property of a deceased person, until she had paid all the money demanded from her.

On Thursday, the 6th, the Sulṭān issued money in lieu of three months' rations to the expeditionary soldiers, in order that they might amply provide themselves. He gave nothing to those remaining behind in Egypt, but left it to the cooks to provide for them in his absence. On that day the Sulṭān sent his tents out to Raidāniyyeh, and his expedition to Syria became a certainty. He announced to the troops in the Maidān that every man who was ready, and had nothing further to detain him, should start before the Sulṭān. Until then the Sulṭān had not hoisted the standard which went in front of the army when they took the field for Syria.

The flag used to be hoisted forty days before departure, but the Sulṭān did not follow in the steps of former kings. On this Thursday the Sulṭān sent 1,000 dīnārs for the expenses of the expedition to the Amīr of the Faithful, Muḥammed al-Mutewekkil 'alā Allāh, by the hand of Ḥusām al-Dīn al-Alwāḥī, gatekeeper of Dahīshah. This was done at the instigation of Amīr Ṭūmān Bai, Grand Dawādār [1]; had it not been for the latter nothing would have been sent him.

The Sulṭān also sent to the four judges to tell them to make ready, but sent them no allowances, a source of much annoyance and inconvenience to them; for since al-Ashraf Bars Bai's expedition to Āmed in A.H. 836 neither the Khalīfah nor the four judges had accompanied the Sulṭān to Syria. But when they did go, it had been the custom to provide them with their expenses. The Sulṭān did not do it on this occasion.

A few days later the Sulṭān sent the Khalīfah a sword inlaid with gold, by one of the officials of the armoury—Muḥammed al-'Ādilī. It has already been mentioned that he sent him a set of new glass. The total amount he had received from the Sulṭān in gifts of gold and other valuables amounted to less than 2,000 dīnārs, and the Khalīfah's preparations for this expedition cost him 5,000 dīnārs or more.

On Friday, the 7th, a large body of the Sulṭān's Memlooks started for Syria, according to orders previously given. A number of troops left barracks but did not start. On that day the successor of Sīdī Aḥmed al-Badawī appeared before the Sulṭān in answer to a summons, who told him to prepare to leave with him for Aleppo. He made excuses that he was in a feeble state of health and was unable to start. This vexed the Sulṭān, who insisted and would accept of no excuse. He also sent to tell the successor of Sīdī Aḥmed al-Rifā'ī, may the blessing of God be upon him, to accompany

[1] "Sous la dynastie des Mamlouks on donnait ce titre à des personnages qui avaient la fonction de faire arriver à leur destination les lettres émanées du Sultan, de lui faire parvenir les placets, et d'introduire les ambassadeurs et autres personnes aux audiences" (Dozy).

"Besides the Grand Dawādār [the Amīr Dawādār al-kabīr] there was also a second Dawādār with the rank of an Amir of 40 Mamlūks, a third with the rank of an Amīr of 20 Mamlūks, and 10 Dawādārs among the bodyguard (khāṣṣikī) in Cairo and in each province. A Dawādār Sikkīn also is frequently mentioned; according to Ibn Iyās's account, his office was to conduct the correspondence between the Sulṭān and his Mamlūks . . ." (M. Sobernheim).

him. Then when the judges felt sure that the Sulṭān was going they set about getting ready, and detailed a large number of deputy judges to accompany them, much to the vexation of the latter. Moreover, the four judges imposed [23] a certain sum of money on each of the deputies, fixed according to each man's station, which raised a fire of indignation against the judges. The Sulṭān also condemned their conduct when he heard of it.

On this day the chief judge of the Shāfiʻī sect, Kemāl al-Dīn al-Ṭawīl, led the people in the Friday prayers; then he asked for and obtained an audience of the Sulṭān, who was then at Dahīshah. At this audience he swore that he had not appropriated any of the money levied on the deputies, but that those of the deputies who had been detailed for the expedition had said: "Let us charge our expenses on the deputies remaining in Egypt." To this the Sulṭān replied: "Do not annoy any of the deputies, nor take them by force, but those who are prepared to go of their own free will, let them go, but use no compulsion." Thus was this odious conduct put a stop to, for which—Praise be to God. A number of deputies had already set about selling their furniture and books, and had incurred losses in consequence of the demand for money.

The like of this did not happen to the judges and their deputies when al-Ashraf Bars Bai set out for Āmed.

On the same date the Sulṭān inspected the household slaves, the Farrāshes, the gatekeepers, the stablemen, the stonemasons, the cellarmen, the armourers, the firemen, and others. He summoned Amīr ʻAlam al-Dīn, who had charge of those who played the drums and fifes, and required him to spend his own money on the men going with him. The Sulṭān said: "You have been living on the proceeds of this office for a number of years, so pay for these men out of your own pocket, otherwise we have some one to succeed you who will do so." Then he paraded the "singers of the bench (?)", namely, Aḥmed Abū Sena, al-Muḥaujib, and al-Maḥlāwī, and ordered them to start with him. He detailed a number of carpenters and stonemasons, inspected them, and issued four months' wages only, without any allowance for rations, saying: "You have been living on State wages for so many years, and when it is my will that you should go on an expedition you ask me for ration allowances."

Meantime, Shems al-Dīn al-Ẓarīf, registrar of the Ḳor'ān readers, selected a number of readers, preachers, and mu'ezzins, and ordered them to proceed with the Sulṭān, as the judges had done with their deputies.

On Sunday, the 9th, 'Ajemī al-Shenḳjī, the Sulṭān's messmate, who had been with elephants to the Governors of Damascus and Aleppo, arrived at the Palace gates; he had been away such a long time that he had been reported dead more than once. It seemed that the Sulṭān had sent him on a secret mission to Shāh Ismā'īl al-Ṣūfī; at least, this was the common talk.

On Tuesday, the 10th of Rebī' al-Ākhir, the Sulṭān's military cortège[1] was ordered to set out from the Maidān before sunrise, and followed the route from the Rumailah by Ḥadarat al-Baḳar and the Ṣalībah.

It consisted of fifteen led dromedaries with gold-embroidered numnahs; three hundred horses, of which [24] a hundred had caparisons of steel chased with gold; and some (of the horses) with velvet of different colours; three horses with gold-embroidered numnahs and saddles inlaid with gold; and three pairs of horses with Bedouin saddles and drums. There were also in the cavalcade twenty-four litters with glossy yellow silk coverings, and two velvet litters on mules also with yellow silk coverings, six treasure cases with

[1] "Ṭulb, pl. Aṭlāb, est, selon Macrizi, un mot qui dans la langue des Curdes désigne un émīr commandant qui a un drapeau roulé et une trompette que l'on sonne au besoin; il a sous ses ordres un nombre de deux cents, cent ou soixante et dix cavaliers. Introduit en Égypte et dans la Syrie sous le règne de Saladin et de ses successeurs, ce terme y a reçu le sens de corps de troupes plus ou moins nombreux, commandé par un officier supérieur, bataillon" (Dozy).

the same hangings; five well-bred horses, two of which carried horse-cloths, gilt stirrups, saddles of crystal and gold mosaic, and drums of crystal and gold; two mares with gold-embroidered horse-cloths, gilt bits, and saddles, the latter with gold hangings ornamented with gold crescents instead of birds.

Riding with the procession were a certain number of Amīrs of Tens wearing muslin turbans, and some eunuch servants, also riding. There were a number of officials, including the Ḳāḍī Maḥmūd Ibn Ajā, Private Secretary; the Ḳāḍī Muḥyi al-Dīn al-Ḳaṣrawi, Inspector of Troops; the Ḳāḍī 'Alā al-Dīn Ibn al-Imām "Nāẓir al-Khāṣ"; the Ḳāḍī Shihāb al-Dīn Aḥmed Ibn al-Jī'ān, Private Secretary; and the Ḳāḍī Abū al-Baḳā, Inspector of Stables; the Ḳāḍī Berekāt Ibn Mūsā, Inspector of Markets; the Ḳāḍī Sharaf al-Dīn al-Ṣaghīr, Secretary of the Memlooks and Government Inspector; and al-Sherefi Yūnus al-Nābulusī, and the Ḳāḍī Kerīm al-Dīn Ibn al-Jī'ān, the princes, and other leading officials. Then came the Royal Standard, the cymbals, and the Sulṭān's and Khalīfah's standards; there were in the procession four drums and four fifes and ten loads of treasure cases—there were usually forty loads.

The Sulṭān's procession went out by the Rumailah Gate, the troops were drawn up, and a vast concourse of people to see it. But when the procession passed the people were not pleased; they thought there were not enough horses, and one who had seen the procession of al-Ashraf Bars Bai when he went to Āmed said that he had 400 gorgeously caparisoned horses with horse-armour, coloured velvet, and steel. Some preferred the procession of Yashbek, the Dawādār (when he went against Shāh Suwār), to that of the Ṣulṭān, giving preference to the former. It went down by the Vizīr's Gate, and came in through the Zawīlah Gate, and went right through Cairo; it was observed as a high day, and all Cairo was in excitement over it.

The procession wound along till it emerged at the

Bāb al-Naṣr, and went on to the royal camp at Raidāniyyeh. On that day the baggage of Amīr al-Mu'minīn al-Mutewekkil 'alā Allāh left, having in front of him two drums and fifes and a trumpeter. Nothing started on that day but the Sulṭān's procession. It was customary of old for the Sulṭān to follow in the rear of the procession, followed again by troops commanded by the Amīrs; but he departed from the customs of former kings in many respects. For instance, he did not hoist the standard over the band quarters as did former kings. They used to hoist the standard, parade the troops, and then make a distribution of money for the expedition; the standard used to fly until the Sulṭān departed, even if it were after an interval of two months.

It was related of al-Ẓāhir Berḳūḳ that when he went out against Tīmūrlenk, his procession left by the Maidān Gate, and that he himself arranged the order of it.

The Sulṭān was mounted carrying an axe in his hand, [25] and rode backwards and forwards from the Maidān Gate to al-Ṣuwwah. It was said that former Sulṭāns departed for Syria when the sun was in the sign of Aries, in early spring, during the moist season. But al-Ghūri left when the heat was extreme and the sun in the sign of Cancer. So the troops suffered great hardships on the journey. Neither was it the ancient custom that the Sulṭān should traverse Cairo on his way out, but that he should go out by Ṣuwwah and traverse Cairo on his return—but this Sulṭān took his own line in everything.

On Thursday, the 13th, it was the common talk that one of the Sulṭān's imported Memlooks named Jānem al-Ifranjī (the European), a rapacious spendthrift (who left with the first detachment of the royal Memlooks before the departure of the Sulṭān), was seizing everything he could lay his hands on, and molesting the people on his way. When the Sulṭān heard of this, he gave orders to the police that he should be arrested and hanged on the spot without trial. It was said that they did arrest him and hang him on a tree at Belbeis in his uniform and wearing his sword, bow, and quiver. They put his servants in irons and brought them to Maḳsharah.

On Friday, the 14th, the Sulṭān came down from the citadel, went to Ḳarāfah, and visited the tombs of the Imām al-Shāfi'ī and the Imām al-Laith, with his son, the Grand Master of the Horse. It was said that the Sulṭān spent a considerable sum in charity on that day. The Sulṭān's baggage and that of the Amīrs left for Raidāniyyeh.

On Saturday, the 15th, the Sulṭān and Malik al-Ashraf Abū al-Naṣr Ḳānṣūh al-Ghūrī left for Syria and Aleppo. It was long since the people had seen a Sulṭān start for these countries in this manner, never since al-Ashraf Bars Bai al-'Alā'ī set out for Āmed, in the year A.H. 836, about 87 years earlier.

On the morning of this Saturday the remainder of the Amīrs assembled with the Sulṭān in the Maidān, in full-dress uniform, and on that day the Sulṭān conferred a robe of honour on Amīr Erkmās Ibn Ṭarā Bai Amīr al-Mejlis and appointed him Keeper of the Armoury, which office had been vacant since the appointment of al-Amīr Sūdūn al-'Ajemī to the office of Atābek.

The number of chief Amīrs who were detailed for personal attendance on the Sulṭān was fifteen ; nine remained behind in Cairo.

* * * * *

[26] At sunrise on Saturday, the 15th, the troops of the Amīrs, forming the Sulṭān's personal escort, moved off in the following order :—

(1) The Corps commanded by Amīr Kurt Bai, one of the chief Amīrs, and formerly Governor of Cairo.

(2) The Corps commanded by Amīr Aḳ Bai al-Ṭawīl, 2nd Master of the Horse, one of the members of the Court.

(3) The Body-guard under Amīr Tāni Bey, the Treasurer.

(4) The Body-guard under Amīr Abrak al-Ashrafi, one of the members of the Court.
(5) The Body-guard under Amīr 'Allān Ibn Ḳarājā, 2nd Dawādār, one of the Court.
(6) The Corps under Amīr Baibars, a relation of the Sulṭān.
(7) The Corps under Amīr Jān Balāṭ, known as Muwattir.
(8) The Corps under Amīr Ḳānṣūh Kurt.
(9) The Corps under Amīr Tamr al-Ḥasanī, known as the Zardkāsh.
(10) The Corps under Amīr Kānṣūh Ibn Sulṭān Chirkes.
(11) The Corps under Amīr Anas Bai Ibn Muṣṭafā, Chief Chamberlain.
(12) The Corps under Amīr Sūdūn Dawādārī, Chief of the Corps of Guards.
(13) The Corps under the Sulṭān's son, al-Nāṣir Muḥammed, Grand Master of the Horse.
(14) The Corps under Amīr Erkmās Ibn Ṭarā Bai Amir Mejlis, who had been appointed Amīr Silāḥ.
(15) The Corps under the Atābek Sūdūn Ibn Jānī Bey, known as al-'Ajemī. His corps was remarkable for splendour and good order.

When the last of these corps had passed the Sulṭān himself left by the Stable Gate near the steps. He was preceded by the royal trumpeter, named Burghashī. The Sulṭān's cavalcade was magnificent; rarely has it been equalled in splendour. At the head of it came the three elephants, gorgeously caparisoned, then came the victorious troops in full-dress uniform, followed by the Amīrs, who were chiefs of the guard, carrying staves with which to keep back the people. After these came the Amīrs of the Ṭablkhānah and all the Amīrs of Tens, then the executive officials.

* * * * *

[27] There were also present in this cavalcade the distinguished brothers of the Sherīf Berekāt, Amīr of Mecca; these went in front of the Chief Amīrs. Then came all the

chief Amīrs, with whom was the Sulṭān's son, His Highness al-Nāṣir, Grand Master of the Horse, and by his side was the Atābek Sūdūn al-'Ajemī. Then followed the four judges of the Shafi'ī Ḥanefī, Mālikī, and Ḥanbalī sects. Then came the Khalīfah, wearing the Baghdād turban with two ribbons, and a Ba'lbec coat with black silk embroidery. He did not have the Khalīfah's flag held above him; he had curtailed many customs observed by former Khalīfahs who were kinsmen of his.

Then came the Sulṭān's led horses, consisting of a pair with sugar-loaf headgear, and saddles with yellow silk coverings and side-drums; another pair had saddle-cloths and gilded saddles with gold-embroidered coverings. Some of the horses had saddles of crystal inlaid with gold, and studded with agate stones, set in silver. A body of chiefs of the Guard followed on foot carrying axes. There were before them neither tents nor royal flute-players as was customary in these royal cavalcades. Then came the baggage and boxes, and the garment cases covered with yellow silk, and the incense-bearer on foot with the censer ahead of him, followed by the Sulṭān al-Malik al-Ashraf Ḳānṣūh al-Ghūri—may he ever be victorious.

He was preceded by the Khalīfah about twenty paces in front of him. The Sulṭān rode a bay horse with numnah and gold saddle, wearing a cap and a white Ba'lbec coat embroidered with a wide border of gold on black silk; it was said to have in it five hundred miskals of gold. That day was one of great splendour, a magnificent sight. The Sulṭān was handsome, and a fine figure in a procession.

Thus the Sulṭān advanced with the royal flag held over him, immediately behind him being the Chief Memlook, Ṣunbul al-'Othmānī. He was accompanied by the armour-bearers in uniform, and a great number of his suite and jemadars.

He entered Cairo by the Zawīlah Gate and passed through
[28] the streets. All Cairo trembled at his presence on that

day, the townsfolk greeted him with prayers for his welfare, and the women cheered him from the windows. The Sulṭān marched in that cavalcade until it came out by the Bāb al-Naṣr Gate, and it was a gala day.

Then the camp at Raidāniyyeh was reached. On the following day chests were brought down containing the gold and silver, each chest containing gold in coin to the amount of 1,000 dīnārs, in addition to other metals. The treasury was depleted of all the money which had been collected since the commencement of this Sulṭān's reign, up to the date of the departure of this expedition. Moreover, a complete clearance was made of all the other storehouses, including articles of intrinsic value and highly wrought weapons collected by former Sulṭāns, gilded saddles inlaid with crystal and agate; also gold-embroidered numnahs, crystal and enamelled drums, embossed sets of horse-armour, gold-embroidered camel saddles, and other royal treasures.

In charge of the chests were a party of treasury clerks and officials in uniform. These chests were borne on fifty camels; then came the armoury borne on a hundred camels, preceded by two drummers and fifers and instruments of military music mounted on camels. All these went on to the camp.

On Sunday, the 16th, the Sulṭān caused it to be proclaimed in Cairo that the army would advance on Friday, the 21st, that every expeditionary soldier must be present on that day, and that no excuse of any kind for absence would be accepted.

When the Sulṭān had established himself in camp, he appointed a number of the deputies of the chief judges to accompany him on the expedition.

* * * * *

[29] He also had with him a great number of builders, carpenters, and blacksmiths, as was customary, and the Chief Sheikh with his troops and flags and drums. He led the Sulṭān's cavalcade on its entry into Damascus, in accordance with the ancient custom on expeditions.

* * * * *

On the 18th, 19th, and 21st there left a number of Amīrs [names omitted] with their Memlooks, said to number 944 men. The Ḳarāniṣah Memlooks, the imported Memlooks, [30] and those born in the country numbered five thousand.

This was the report; Heaven only knows the truth of it.

It was said that some two thousand of the Ḳarāniṣah Memlooks, with the unfit, the Sheikhs, the Imported Memlooks, and those born in the country, remained behind in Cairo, in the barracks and in the citadel.

While the Sulṭān was in camp at Raidāniyyeh, a letter arrived from the Governor of Aleppo, telling him that Ibn 'Othmān had sent a messenger with a letter, which he now forwarded to the Sulṭān by the same messenger. It was expressed in pleasant terms to the following purport. After calling the Sulṭān his father and offering prayers for his welfare, Ibn 'Othmān asserted that he had not encroached upon the dominions of 'Alī Dōlāt except with his (the Sulṭān's) permission, and that he had rebelled against him. That it was he who had stirred up the ancient hostility between his father (Ibn 'Othmān's ?) and the Sulṭān Ḳāit Bai, which led to what had happened, and had caused the greatest mischief in his (the Sulṭān's) country, so that his death was entirely justified. As to Ibn Suwār, who had succeeded 'Alī Dōlāt, if the Sulṭān thought fit to retain him, or to replace him, the matter rested entirely with him. As to the merchant importers of Circassian Memlooks, Ibn 'Othmān said he had not stood in their way, but that they had complained of their treatment as regards their payment in gold and silver, and had refused to bring the Memlooks over. He further said that he was prepared to return to the Sulṭān the dominions he had taken from 'Alī Dōlāt, and would do whatever the Sulṭān desired.

Upon this the Sulṭān summoned the leading Amīrs and read to them Ibn 'Othmān's letter, the contents of which greatly pleased both them and the Sulṭān and aroused in their minds a feeling that peace and an early return to their homes were at hand.

But as facts showed later, this was nothing but a piece of trickery and deception on the part of Ibn 'Othmān in order to achieve his objects.

The next day there arrived in Cairo the Amīr Īnāl Bai, Dawādār Sikkīn, who had gone to Aleppo to obtain news of Ibn 'Othmān. On his arrival he found that the Sulṭān had already started on the expedition, and had left Cairo. He reported that Ibn 'Othmān's messenger had arrived at Aleppo, that he was desirous of peace, and had sent numerous presents to Īnāl Bai there.

As to the Sulṭān's doings in camp, the night of his departure from Raidāniyyeh he conferred a robe on Ṭūmān Bai, the Dawādār, and appointed him Regent in Cairo during his absence. He also conferred a robe of honour on the Ḳāḍī Berekāt Ibn Mūsā, and appointed him Inspector of Markets in the place of Amīr Māmāī during his absence. He made Zeinī Berekāt Ibn Mūsā adviser on all Imperial questions.

On the same night lighted torches were brought, and a spark blew from them on to the Sulṭān's tent, and one side of it was burnt; the people did not regard this as a good omen for the Sulṭān.

[31] When Zeinī Berekāt Ibn Mūsā entered Cairo he became a most important personage. He represented the Sulṭān, and became controller of the affairs of the country, and the Amīr Dawādār Kebīr was as a screw in his hand to be turned what way he would.

On that night the Sulṭān also conferred a robe of honour on Amīr Elmās, appointing him Governor of Cairo, charging him with its protection and to abstain from tyranny. He gave a robe of honour to the Amīr Māmāī, the Inspector of Markets, and ordered him to go with him to Aleppo. The Amīr Dawādār left the Sulṭān's presence and returned to Cairo, passing through the Ṣalībah [1] with a great cavalcade,

[1] A "Ṣalībah" is a technical name for an Egyptian irrigation bank.

with criers in front of him proclaiming security to the people and the continuance of trade. No one was to walk about in the evening carrying arms; the molestation of tradesmen by Memlooks and slaves was forbidden. Men were to come for redress of grievances to the Gate of the Dawādār; the people shouted and made prayers for him. The Dawādār was beloved by the people and by the poor, and rarely did harm to anyone. Thus he made his way along the Ṣalībah, in the midst of a great cavalcade with runners and water-carriers and crowds of people—with the royal followers and Memlooks in front of him, and made his way to the residence. Then I said:—

Creation has been honoured by the Regent, whose word is law;
Noble, brave in the fields of battle, a fine horseman,
Victorious in battle with sword and lance.
If a wronged one complains to him of his wrongs,
The light of his justice arises for him,
Promising that morning will appear;
Lord, be his helper and protector in all the changes and chances of this life,
And spare Ibn Mūsā to his subjects;
A second Moses, pure-hearted, a security against sorcery,
A noble gentleman, then Inspector of Markets, he was born on the night of al-Ḳadr.
On account of his godliness he has regard for the noble Seyyids,
And thus obtained a great heavenly reward;
He has become Director of the Food supplies,
The point of his lance pierces the necks of his enemies.
A Pharaoh in Egypt, he has acquired the fortune of Yūsuf.
I seek protection for him through the Sūrahs of the Ḳor'ān,
After the Stars, the Light, and the Day of Resurrection.

On Saturday, the 22nd, the Sulṭān left the royal camp at Raidāniyyeh, accompanied by the Khalīfah, the four judges, his son, His Highness al-Nāṣir, Grand Master of the Horse, and Aḳ Bai al-Ṭawīl, Second Master of the Horse.

He said the morning prayers and left for Khānḳāh Siriāḳūs, having remained seven days in the camp. He halted a day and a night at the monastery of Siriāḳūs, and left on Sunday, the 23rd. On Monday, the 24th, a third instalment of wages was issued to the troops who had stayed behind in Egypt. Amīr Ṭaḳṭ Bai sat at the steps, and the wages were distributed in his presence; it was the first payment of wages in the absence of the Sulṭān. The same day the Amīr Dawādār gave orders to the leading Amīrs whom the Sulṭān had appointed to the Sharḳīeh and Gharbīeh provinces to leave for their posts, and to protect the countries from devastation by the Arabs. So Tānī Bey left for the Sharḳīeh and Ezbek, the gunner, for the Gharbīeh province. Al-Amīr Ḳānṣūh al-Fājir went to Menūfiyyeh, al-Amīr Ḳānṣūh Abū Sena to [32] al-Buḥairah. Bakhsh Bai had gone to the Fayyūm to see about the construction of a dam there.

Then the Dawādār issued a proclamation in Cairo to all the Royal Memlooks who had been detailed for the Dominions that they should accompany these Amīrs, and that none should remain behind, and they complied with his orders.

On Monday, the 24th, Amīr Naurūz, Tājir al-Memālīk, one of the Amīrs of the Ṭablkhānah died. He was originally one of Ashraf Ḳāit Bai's Memlooks. He had become very big and heavy, and was so fat he could hardly move, and he remained in this condition until he died.

It was reported that the Sulṭān bestowed upon his Memlook Māmāī, whom he appointed to the Censorship, the baggage of Naurūz, his horses, mules, and tents. At least, that was what was commonly said.

The same day the sky became black with clouds, there was thunder, lightning, and torrents of rain. This happened on the 1st of the Coptic month Baunah. The rain continued for three days on end; it was considered quite a marvel. This was succeeded by violent winds and the sky became quite yellow at sunset. The people drew evil omens from this, of revolutions, which actually did take place later on. The same day news came from the Sulṭān that when he started from the monastery a man was found in his tent who was thought to be an assassin, sent by 'Alam al-Dīn, the Sulṭān's barber, who had incurred his displeasure, as previously mentioned. The enemies of 'Alam al-Dīn said that he had sent that fanatic to kill the boy named 'Abd al-Razzāḳ, who had become barber to the Sulṭān in the stead of 'Alam al-Dīn. The man, who was thought to be a fanatic, was arrested and brought before the Sulṭān, who tried to make him confess, but he denied and was ordered to be hanged.

Then the Sulṭān sent to Elmās, Governor of Cairo, to arrest 'Alam al-Dīn and his relations, and to hang him on his own gate. When 'Alam al-Dīn heard of this he fled from his home and hid himself. Then the Vālī arrested a number of Syces who were relations of 'Alam al-Dīn and put them in irons. Some said that they had been hanged in Maḳsharah, or imprisoned till the Sulṭān should return.

Previous to this stores of chaff and bran belonging to the Amīrs had been burnt to the value of about two thousand dīnārs. This was put down to some of the Syces, relations of 'Alam al-Dīn the barber—for if an animal is once down every one digs his knife into him. Persistent search was made for 'Alam al-Dīn the barber's capture, and it was said that the Vālī, on the flight of 'Alam al-Dīn, sent his Memlooks, in full uniform, to search for him, but without success.

On Friday, the 28th of Rebī' al-Ākhir, the Dawādār left in order to see about repairing the dams at al-Faiḍ and Abū Manjā, which the guardians had failed to block up. The Nile had risen before orders had been issued on the subject, and had reached a height of 12 cubits. The Dawādār took the utmost trouble to close the sluices, boats were broken up under these two sluices, and still the water was uncontrolled; till at last God came to the rescue, and the Nile receded.

During the month of Jumādā al-ūlā, Amīr Māmāī al-Ṣaghīr, the Inspector of Markets, joined the Sulṭān. He had with him a little lad of 13 called Ḳāsim Ibn Aḥmed Bey Ibn Abū Yazīd Ibn 'Othmān, nephew of Selīm Shāh Ibn 'Othmān.

When the latter's brother, Aḥmed Bey (the boy's father), was killed, his son Ḳāsim fled with his tutor, and went to Aleppo in disguise, and then came to Egypt and lived there until the [33] Sulṭān left for Syria, when he took him with him for reasons of his own, but no good came of it. The lad went out with Māmāī, with led horses before him. Moreover, the Sulṭān had provided him with an outfit and about 2,000 dīnārs, hoping that the boy's fame might be heard of in the Dominions of Ibn 'Othmān, and that it might be said that there was one of Ibn 'Othmān's family in Egypt, a male child. The Sulṭān thought that the troops of Ibn 'Othmān, on hearing this, would desert and come over to him, but nothing came of it.

The lad Ḳāsim passed along the Ṣalībah wearing a Turkoman turban, a royal dagger in his belt, and was said to have a ruby ear-ring. He was accompanied by a number of Osmanlis, Amīr Māmāī, and Īnāl Bai. The latter was Dawādār Sikkīn, who had come from Syria, and had been ordered by the Sulṭān to return a second time, and to go with him to Aleppo.

Amongst the things that happened during the absence of the Sulṭān, Amīr Elmās, Governor of the Police, took to making levies on the people for the construction of roads in various quarters. They made one road at the top of the Bran Market, one in Ḥusseiniyyeh, and another over Ḳanṭarah al-Ḥājib. A road was also made at Farāyīn, and at al-Maḳs, and several others elsewhere, and they blocked up a number of the wicket gates in Cairo. He ordered a lamp to be hung up outside every shop, and none were to leave their houses after dark, nor to carry arms. It was a matter of interest that the Dawādār did not disturb any of the Aulād al-Nās, nor compel them to live in the citadel during the Sulṭān's absence.

It was customary, when the Sulṭān went to Syria, for the guardians of the citadel to tyrannize over the Aulād al-Nās and to compel them to spend every night in the citadel. This was an annoyance, and an extreme fatigue to the men, having to climb up every night, and a long way from their homes in the winter. Any man who failed to go himself had to provide a substitute. This was done till the days of Ashraf Ḳāit Bai. It was recorded amongst the good acts of the Dawādār, and the people blessed him for abolishing this odious custom.

Another incident in the Sulṭān's absence was that one of the imported Memlooks wanted to buy corn from a ship by the river bank and could not find a porter. Finding one of the fellāḥīn of the Ṣa'īd with a donkey and a sack, he tried to take them from him. This led to a quarrel, during which the Memlook struck the fellāḥ a severe blow on the head which drew blood, and the man threw himself into the river and was drowned. This brought a crowd round the Memlook, whom they seized and took to the Dawādār's house, where he was put in irons and sent to the Vālī. When his comrades heard of this they went to the Dawādār's house; they found he was away at the dam of al-Faiḍ seeing about its being [34] blocked up. The Memlooks were told that the Dawādār had handed over the Memlook to Elmās the Vālī. Thereupon a great number of the imported Memlooks came down from their quarters with a view to plundering and burning the Vālī's house and releasing the Memlook. The Dawādār, however, took no further notice of that murder, and no more was heard of it.

The following event took place during the absence of the Sulṭān: One of the eunuchs named 'Amber, chief of the Ashrafi order, who lived in the ruins of Tatar (?), and was supposed to be wealthy (?), and had in his possession consignments of pay for the Memlooks, was attacked at night, whilst asleep in his house, by thieves, who beat him on the head with jelabahs till he died. They carried off everything, and killed his male and female slave, making no disturbance whatever. Amīr Ṭakṭ Bai, Governor of the Citadel, was completely at a loss to understand how this could have happened right in the heart of the citadel, when the gates were locked after sunset; it was considered quite an extraordinary occurrence.

On Tuesday, the 9th, a chief Ḳāḍī of the Shāfi'ī sect died;

he was called Ḳalḳashandī. May the Lord have mercy upon him! He was a holy man of learning and excellence, well versed in the traditions. He filled the office of Ḳāḍī twice during the reign of Ashraf al-Ghūrī. He was very old, nearly 90; he was one of the most distinguished scholars of the Shāfiʿī sect. May God have mercy upon him!

On the same day came news of the arrival of the Sulṭān at Ṣāliḥiyyeh on Tuesday, the 25th Rebīʿ al-Ākhir, and it was said that when about to leave there he gave permission to the Khalīfah and the four judges to go forward as far as Gazah.

When he reached Ḳaṭīyā[1] he was met by Amīr Ḳānṣūh Rajlah, Governor of Ḳaṭīyā, where he was hospitably entertained and given (it was said) many presents.

Amongst stories circulated during the march was that a mule belonging to the Ḥanefī Ḳāḍī was stolen, but was recovered with the aid of a gift; also that a bundle containing the Ḥanbalī Ḳāḍī's clothes was stolen from his tent; and that a camel laden with money belonging to the Sulṭān was stolen, but the culprits were arrested, and three camel-drivers were cut in two. None of these reports were verified.

Then came news of the entry of the Sulṭān into Gazah on Thursday, the 4th, where he was met by the Governor, Amīr Dōlāt Bai, hospitably entertained, and offered numerous presents. He was said to have stayed there five days, and then to have moved on.

The Sulṭān when at Gazah was said to have decorated Jemāl al-Dīn al-Alwāḥī, Janitor of Dahīshah, and to have appointed him chief teacher in the place of Shihābī Aḥmed Ibn Ṭūlūnī, who had been removed from that office, This appointment may be regarded as one of the mistakes of the time, he being unsuitable for the post.

On Friday, the 19th, came Ibn Abū al-Raddād with news that the Nile was found, on measurement, to have reached 12 cubits, which was considered extraordinary, within

[1] The town still exists on the road to Palestine.

6 cubits of a full Nile, according to Maḳrīzī in his topographical dictionary; Sheikh Suyūṭī, in his book entitled *Kaukab al-Rauḍat*, gave it as 24 inches more. Since the time of Nāṣir Muḥammed Ibn Ḳalāūn it had not been known to reach 12 cubits; during his time, in the year A.H. 761, it did reach 12 cubits. The full Nile was on the 6th of Misra. The rise [35] in that year reached nearly 24 cubits; the people suffered considerable loss in consequence, and prayed for its fall. It eventually subsided at the end of the month Tūt. During the reign of Ashraf Bars Bai, in the year A.H. 838, the Nile rose 11 cubits 10 inches, and reached its full height on the 2nd of Misra. The people thought that the Nile would cover the land during the sowing season, beyond its proper time; but everything turned out prosperously that year, and the Nile reached its maximum height at the proper time. Mention will be made of this in its own place.

On Saturday, the 27th, the death occurred of Amīr Jānī Bey; he was one of the Amīrs entitled to a band, and was one of the Memlooks of Ashraf Ḳāit Bai; he was an excellent man.

In the same month a new coinage was issued and the old one cancelled. The value of the old coins was proclaimed at two Niṣfs to the Raṭl, and that of the new coins as marked upon them. The affairs of the people came to a standstill.

On Tuesday, the 1st, a number of Deputy Judges and nobles proceeded to the Dawādār's house to offer him their congratulations on the new month.

News came of the Sulṭān's entry into Damascus on Tuesday, the 8th; he was met by Amīr Bars Bai, Governor of Syria. The Sulṭān entered with a numerous cavalcade, preceded by the Khalīfah, the four judges, and the chief Amīrs, the Amīrs of Ṭablkhānāh, the Amīrs of Tens, the principal office-holders, the executive officials, a strong body of troops, and many others.

He was met by the Amīrs and troops of Syria. He had over his head the dome-shaped umbrella as used by ancient kings. The city of Damascus was splendidly decorated in his honour, and the trumpets of good tidings were sounded for him in the citadel. Certain European merchants showered gold and silver over his head, and Sī Bai spread silk hangings for his horse to walk over. But the Memlooks so crowded upon him in their greed for the gold and silver that the Sulṭān nearly fell off his horse, so much was he jostled by the people. So he stopped the scattering of gold and silver and the spreading of silk hangings under his horse's feet. It was in truth a gala day in Damascus, one to be long remembered. The procession made its way into Damascus by the Gate of Victory, out into the open plain as far as the Stone Seat (Maṣṭabah), known as the Sulṭān's Stone Seat, at Ḳābūn al-Ḳāḳūni. The Sulṭān ordered one of his chamberlains to rebuild it, as it had fallen to pieces through lapse of time.

There had not been a procession on this scale between the days of Ashraf Bars Bai, when he went to Syria in the year A.H. 836, and that of Malik al-Ashraf Ḳānṣūh al-Ghūrī.

The Sulṭān spent nine days at the Maṣṭabah at al-Ḳābūn. It was said that Ḳāḍī Kemāl al-Dīn al-Ṭawīl preached at the Mosque of Benī Umeyyah on two Fridays, and that the Sulṭān did not attend the Friday prayers there. The decorations at Damascus were kept up for seven days; after that the Sulṭān started for Ḥomṣ, and then moved thence and went to [36] Ḥamāh. He was there met by the Governor Jān Birdī al-Ghazālī, who was said to have entertained him in an even more princely fashion than did the Amīr of Damascus. According to rumour the Sulṭān quartered there Ḳāsim Bey Ibn Aḥmed Ibn 'Othmān, previously mentioned as having started with Amīr Māmāī, the Inspector of Markets, from Egypt.

It was said that on Monday night, the 14th of this month, there was a terrible eclipse of the moon,[1] the earth being completely darkened. The eclipse lasted more than fifty minutes; the entire orb of the moon was darkened, and remained so till the last third of the night.

On Monday, the 14th, the Dawādār gave orders for an

[1] See Oppolzer's *Canon der Mondfinsternisse*, p. 367, where this eclipse is recorded.

Arab criminal to be hanged on the Ḳanṭarah al-Ḥājib. The affairs of Egypt were extremely well directed by the Dawādār during the Sulṭān's absence. He instructed Amīr Elmās, Governor of Cairo, to patrol the streets of the town every night after dark, and a hundred of the imported Memlooks were detailed for the purpose to patrol by turns with the Vālī till daybreak. Thus good order was maintained during the absence of the Sulṭān, contrary to the usual experience. The Dawādār was constantly reproaching Elmās the Vālī for impressing people to maintain the roads; it was a most tyrannical practice. He arranged with the police and the watchmen to levy contributions on the citizens for the repair of the roads, and they used to collect a considerable amount in this way. The watchmen would stop at a certain man's house and demand what money they thought fit, and if the owner ran away they used to nail up the door and fasten his children and family inside till he came and paid them what they demanded. They would fasten a widow-woman in her house, and leave her without food or drink till she threw them from the window a blanket, mattress, or carpet, or something of the kind. They used to levy on the poor the payment of an Ashrafi or two, and from those in good circumstances in some cases five, in others ten, Ashrafis as they chose. This they did in the Khaṭṭ al-Maks, Khaṭṭ Bāb al-Baḥr, the Milk Market, al-Ḥuseinīya, the Bran Market, Khaṭṭ Birkah al-Raṭlī, and other places; in this way they exercised a tyranny exceeding that of Huniādes, on the pretext that the construction of roads was for the good of the Muḥammedans. Much money was gathered, and but little spent. So Sī Bai determined that a collection should be made from Seyyidah Nefīsah to the end of Ibn Ṭūlūn's market-place on all property and shops in that locality. It was supposed that they would construct a wall to prevent a surprise attack by the Arabs. But all this was a trick to obtain the people's money. They began to make lists of the properties and shops in the quarter of Ṭūlūn and Karāfah.

When the Dawādār learnt that Elmās was committing these acts of oppression in his name, he swore a great oath that he had had no knowledge of it, and put a stop to these dreadful doings, gaining thereby the thanks of all the people.

Then the Memlooks in the employ of the Chamberlain tried to start [37] another piece of tyranny. They collected a good deal of money from the residents of Birkah al-Raṭlī in order to cut through the bar across the mouth of the lake, which had greatly increased in height, so much so that it prevented the passage of ships into the lake. When the Dawādār got news of this, he put a stop to this also, and ordered the entrance to be completely blocked up to prevent ships from entering.

On Saturday, the 19th, the Dawādār returned; he had been to the Fayyūm to inspect the embankment which Amīr Bakhsh Bai had built there. During the Sulṭān's absence the Dawādār used to ride out every day accompanied by the Amīrs of Tens, who were still in Egypt, towards Maṭariyyeh and Birkah al-Ḥāj; he used to return by the Naṣr Gate, preceded by very many Amīrs and soldiers. This was done with the express object of preventing the Arabs and fellāḥīn from thinking that Egypt was denuded of troops; it was a well-conceived idea.

On Monday, the 21st, corresponding to the 27th of Abīb, the Nile was at its fullest. The artificial dam was cut on the 22nd, corresponding to the 28th of Abīb. It had reached its full height four days before the month Misra. The Nile had only once before been known to reach its fullest as early as the 27th of Abīb, in the year A.H. 845. When the Nile was in full flood, Amīr Ṭūmān Bai, the Dawādār and the Regent went to cut the dam in a rowing boat (?), proceeded to the Nilometer, and anointed the column.

He then left the Nilometer in the rowing-boat, accompanied by a number of leading Amīrs—Ṭakṭ Bai, Governor of the Citadel, Amīr Erzamak, Nāshif, and others. When the dam was cut the Dawādār returned home with a great procession, preceded by the Amīrs in full dress, and many of the leading officials. As soon as the dam was cut the water poured with tremendous force into the basins. The people rejoiced that day that the Nile had reached its height, before its usual time. And someone said: "Enjoy the water of the Nile before its inundation; a draught of its water is as good as medicine to us; its sweetness has without doubt come in floods."

Amongst the events of this time was the Dawādār's putting a stop to people residing on the embankment at Birkah al-Raṭlī and all the creeks. He made a bridge over the Zarībah canal, the wharf at which the plaster was unloaded. So the business of the Middle Island fell into decay, not a house remained, not a shop was opened. He prevented the gamblers from putting up a gaming-house, either on the embankment or along the Zarībah. The houses of Birkah al-Raṭlī fell into ruins, especially those of the children of al-Jī'ān, the house of the Private Secretary, and other houses of the well-to-do classes suffered likewise. All the owners suffered much hardship this year in consequence and lost the rent of their houses. [38] It was said that Khaukhat al-Jisr (Bridge Lane) was to be shut up.

The Ḳāḍī Berekāt Ibn Mūsa, the Inspector of Markets, besought the Dawādār to allow the ships to enter as usual and to let the people live on the embankment; but he refused, saying that the people would corrupt the wives of the gentlemen who came with the Sulṭān for the ceremony of the opening of the Nile.

He kept firmly to his decision; then towards the end of the Nile functions he made a concession to the Ḳāḍī Berekāt Ibn Mūsā that five ships belonging to dealers might be admitted to the lake as usual; so the confectioner, the cheese-monger, the fruiterer, the vegetable-seller, and the (Sūwīkhati?) entered, and no others. These men, after remaining for some days moving about here and there and not finding anybody to trade with, left again, and the Birkah al-Raṭlī became quite deserted; there was no one there even to kindle a fire. This formed the subject of an elegy by Sheikh Bedr al-Dīn al-Zeitūnī :—

I asked the Lord of Heaven to grant victory to our Sulṭān,
Al-Ghūrī, the Father of Victory, the esteemed King,
Most noble, invincible, Defender of the True Faith, of perfect dignity.
A feeling of desolation came over the creation at his absence ;
Here is the Birkah al-Raṭlī shedding tears ; we can rightly bewail the loss of pleasant places,
Especially the covered places and her fair banks ;
There the light-hearted could meet,
And assuredly companionship is better than loneliness.
There the sweet, shady sycamore grew,
The birds and the beasts of the field have mourned over her,
The streams have shed bitter tears and cried out in anguish of heart
At the calamity that has happened to the Bridge.
Its lofty tree weeps tears of blood in its mosque ;
The Syrian is mourning over the granaries,
The houses along the banks are deserted and tenantless,
Her palaces are void, and, oh ! how lovely are the people with empty palaces.
Lament with much grief and lamentation over Birkah al-Raṭlī,
Over the punishment and loss that has befallen her ;
The shipowners used to take delight in her ;
There the fruiterer hastened with his ship bearing plums and pomegranates,
Flowers of many kinds, white roses, lilies, and myrtles, greeted with beaming faces ;
There came also the cheese-maker, cooking on board, joining fire to water on the stream ;
For the eaters there were thirsty confectioneries,
The thirst of which was quenched with cloud-water.
The pistachio-tree gave splendour to her open spaces,
And her sugar records the tradition of Abū Dharr ;
There the opium-eater was in constant delight,
But since the curtailment of his joys he has been engrossed in anxious thought ;

There the drunkard was in the height of enjoyment, passing round the wine-goblets on the night of the full moon.
There were the ships, decked or open, for passengers ;
Reciters of verse came thither with players of musical instruments,
And lutes sounding softly like the turtle dove.
[39] Now time has obliterated all those resorts,
Crows and owls in their nests mourn over them ;
The anemone has cast its petals there,
The tender branches of the trees have shed their foliage,
The blackbird has donned his sombre robes ;
There is heard the sound of water as the river beats against the bank,
The clouds shed tears, and the dawn is as the beginning of the night,
The noonday sun is darkened, and the full moon eclipsed till dawn.
Our Middle Island has become a waste
From the damming up of the water,
They have taken away its falling timbers for sale,
And left nothing but the bare walls ;
The boatmen are in dire distress,
There is no means of livelihood nor ship-owner ;
They have sold their deck-coverings and sails,
The oars have vanished—none knows whither,
O eyes, shed copious tears of grief !
O heart, patiently endure !
God's favour be on the days that passed so joyfully, when we in Egypt were in security.
The Dawādār it was who issued these prohibitions,
With intent to protect the women who came out with the Sulṭān,
And the purdah girls, in the early morning,
To protect the wives and daughters of the people from misfortune ;
By giving these orders he was the most noble protector of the wives and daughters of all people from trouble.
Had it not been for the intercession of Mūsā,
For which he has received thanks and rewards,

The dealers' ships would not have been allowed to enter,
Nor would anyone have appeared on the embankments.
Oh, Lord, grant victory for our Sulṭān and the Army of Egypt!
Grant them a safe return to their nation and country,
We pray for the chosen one Muḥammed of the family of Hāshim,
To guide to all goodness and felicity,
Likewise blessings be on his family and companions and on the next generation
And perfect grace be given them on the Day of Resurrection;
May the mercy of God be upon them
As long as the morning breeze blows over the branches
And the turtle-dove cooes.

And the versifier, al-'Aufī, prays for all who discover a fault of Zeitūni's, and graciously draw a veil over it.

On Friday, the 26th, Sheikh Tāj al-Dīn al-Dhākir died. May God have mercy on him! He was one of the chief Ṣūfī Sheikhs, well known among the people for his justice and uprightness, in fact a guileless man.

In the month of Rejeb Amīr Ṭarā Bey died, one of the Amīrs of Tens. On the first of the month, which fell on a Thursday, a number of deputy judges, noblemen, and clerks went to the Dawādār's house to wish him good luck in the new month. On Thursday, the 8th, Taghrī Birdi, known as Shemshamānī, died. He claimed to be one of the Amīrs of Tens; it was said that he was once a water-carrier; he died the owner of land and property. He was rich, but was said to have been avaricious and miserly.

The same day came news of the death of one of the Amīrs [40] of Tens called Musāyed, who was on active service with the Sulṭān. He was originally one of Ashraf Ḳāit Bai's Memlooks.

On this day the Amīrs who had been in the Sharḳīeh and Gharbīeh provinces returned. At this time also, the people were troubled by the new coinage. Goods were sold at two prices, a silver niṣf became equal to 16 dirhems of the old coinage; the new coins were reckoned by number, they were extremely light, and the people suffered in consequence, and shops were closed for the same reason. Bread and other necessaries went up in price, which almost brought about a famine.

Then came news of the Sulṭān's arrival at Aleppo, which he had entered on Thursday the 10th of Jumādā al-Ākhira, which day was observed as a high day and holiday.

The Sulṭān was preceded by the Khalīfah, the four judges, and other Amīrs as in his Syrian procession. The canopy of the royal parasol was carried over his head by Khāir Bey, chief of the Amīrs, Viceroy of Aleppo, as Sī Bai, the Governor of Damascus, had done.

As soon as the Sulṭān had entered Aleppo, emissaries arrived from Selīm Shāh Ibn 'Othmān, Emperor of Constantinople. It was said that he sent his military judge, a person named Rukn al-Dīn, and one of his Amīrs called Ḳarājā Pasha with 700 dependants to Aleppo, and I have it on written authority that the Sulṭān on seeing the Ḳāḍī of Ibn 'Othmān and Ḳarājā Pasha abused them for Ibn 'Othmān's action towards him, more especially for his taking possession of the dominions of 'Alī Dōlāt. In reply the Ḳāḍī and Ḳarājā Pasha said that their master had commissioned them to negotiate a peace, and that they were ordered to comply with the Sulṭān's wishes without further reference to him. But this was mere bluff and trickery to prevent the Sulṭān's going to war, and to shake his determination—which was borne out by subsequent events.

Then Ibn 'Othmān's Ḳāḍī produced legal opinions from the learned men of their country, who had pronounced the death of Shāh Ismā'īl as justified by the sacred law. Moreover, Ibn 'Othmān wrote to the Sulṭān in this wise: "Thou art my Father and I ask thee to pray for me, but do not come between me and the Ṣūfī."

Another piece of deceit practised by Ibn 'Othmān (towards the Sulṭān al-Ghūrī) was his asking for sugar and sweetmeats, in response to which demand al-Ghūrī sent him a hundred Ḳinṭārs of sugar and sweetmeats in large boxes. Ibn

'Othmān also wrote that nothing could deter him from wiping off Ismā'īl Shah from the face of the earth, "but do not," he said, "let this prevent peace between you and me." He tried to give the impression that he was making war against the Sūfī, but this was not his real object. They said that when he was at Ḳaisāriyyeh he was about to march against the Ṣūfī. Then the Sulṭān presented Ibn 'Othmān's emissaries with robes of honour.

Ibn 'Othmān was said to have sent al-Ghūrī many presents, also to the Khalīfah and to Amīr Sūdūn al-'Ajemī. Amongst these were forty Memlooks, furs, suits of velvet and serge, Ba'lbec costumes, and other things. To the Khalīfah he sent two furs, a velvet suit with cuffs of gold thread, and two suits of superfine serge. Ibn 'Othmān's military judge also gave him two suits of serge, a prayer-carpet, and a mule. The Sulṭān also sent splendid presents to Amīr Kebīr, including furs, velvet, and serge clothing and two slaves.

After this the Sulṭān deputed Amīr Moghul Bey Dawādār [41] Sikkīn to proceed to Ibn 'Othmān with a letter containing the conditions of peace.

Meanwhile his army halted awaiting the reply. I composed the following verses about the Sulṭān's expedition from the time of his departure from Egypt up to his entry into Aleppo. Then I said :—

Offer up prayers for victory for our noble king, Sulṭān of Egypt,
His departure for Syria, Damascus, and the Land of Beauty,
Has the Divine sanction.
He decided to reconnoitre the country,
And it forthwith opened its bounty to him.
Its governors came to meet him in willing submission,
The keen-edg'd sword was not drawn against him.
Had Alexander the Great been alive among mankind,
He would have honoured him and paid him all courtesy,
His epoch surpassed that of all kings in splendour ;
So listen thou and hear without more ado.
I saw him when he passed by with the cavalcade,
Mightier than Barḳūḳ, who himself was an Ashrafī,

The Khalīfah and the judges rode before him,
The serpents hid themselves from his armies;
I put him under the protection of the verses of the Sūrah of Yūsuf;
And his troops under the protection of the verses of the Sūrah of "the ornaments of gold".
Thursday was the day of his entry into Gazah with his army;
Damascus exclaimed in her joy at his coming,
"Welcome to the just king of men."
The brow of Rubwah glowed with light
When Joseph's encampment (i.e. Saladin's) decked itself with flowers;
Ḥámāh came under the protection of his justice,
The Orontes forthwith obeyed him without demur,
The Euphrates yearned for him and came on in full flood,
Aleppo was cheered by his arrival,
But Egypt was desolate at his departure;
Aleppo was honoured by him and said "O, joy!
Hail to the graceful newcomer."
Our Sulṭān al-Ghūri felt strongly supported,
Since the All-merciful encircled him with his secret favour.
May God preserve him for ever,
As long as the Zephyr intoxicates like wine.
These are the feeble verses of Ibn Iyās.
May all blessings fall on the Holy Prophet,
The best of mankind and the greatest of helpers,
On his family and kindred—as long as the night
Covers with its darkness, and the day dawns.

It was related that the Sulṭān on his entry into Aleppo gave instruction to Ḳāḍī Kemāl al-Dīn Ṭawīl to deliver an oration in the grand mosque of Aleppo. A great congregation assembled. The Ḳāḍī ascended the pulpit and preached an eloquent sermon, quoting sacred traditions in favour of peace.

The Muezzins also called in the mosques, and the Sulṭān's portions of the Ḳor'ān were read. Preachers delivered sermons, and it was observed as [42] a high day in their mosque. The Sulṭān did not attend, nor was he present at Friday's prayers, as he had been at Damascus, for which he was blamed. Ḳāḍī Kemāl al-Dīn preached in the large mosque during the Sulṭān's stay at Aleppo. According to accounts of the Sulṭān's doings there he made Ḳānṣūh the Viceroy of Aleppo, an Amīr of a thousand, also Yūsuf al-Nāṣirī the superintendent of the buttery, who had been deputy of Ḥamāh, and Ṭarā Bai Deputy of Ṣafad, and Tamrāz Deputy of Tripoli. He also distributed thirty dīnārs each to the camp-followers who had accompanied him without subsistence allowance. He originally meant to give fifty dīnārs, but a protest was made by the Secretary of the Memlooks, and he reduced it to thirty.

To the troops he gave three months' ration money. Then the Sulṭān issued to the imported Memlooks a number of arms from the citadel stores at Aleppo, also innumerable horses. Moreover, he continued giving them large presents of money, well-bred horses, and weapons on the road, but he did not give anything to the Ḳarāniṣah Memlooks, which offended them greatly.

The Sulṭān read the Khatmah on the Great Maidān at Aleppo on Thursday and Thursday night. There were present the Amīr of the Faithful al-Mutewekkil 'alā Allāh, the four judges, and the Sheikhs of the Monasteries. The Amīr of the Faithful prayed with the Sulṭān in his tent afternoon and evening. On that day the Sulṭān gave away 400 dīnārs and 100 head of sheep. He presented to the Ḳāḍī of the Shafi'īs 70 dīnārs, and to his deputies and 'Ulemās 70 dīnars, a similar amount also to the Ḥanefī Ḳāḍī.

The Mālikī Ḳāḍī received 50 dīnārs and his three deputies 30, and to the Ḥanbali Ḳāḍī he allowed a similar sum. He also conferred on the Sheikhs 50 dīnārs each ; on the poor who had come with him he bestowed 10 dīnārs each. To the readers of Aleppo who were present at the Khatmah and others he gave 5 dīnārs each.

After that the Sulṭān summoned the Amīrs of Thousands, and their deputies, the Amīrs of the Ṭablkhānāh, and Amīrs of Tens, and made them swear on the Ḳor'ān that they would not betray him. He gave orders for the parade of the troops in the Maidān of Aleppo in full dress; they were made to pass under two crossed swords, after the custom of the Turks, who regard this as a most sacred oath.

Then the Sulṭān sent for Ḳāsim Bey from Ḥamāh, and conferred a robe of honour on him. After this news reached Aleppo that Selīm Shāh Ibn 'Othmān had arrested the Sulṭān's emissary, Amīr Moghul Bai, one of the Dawādārs, and put him in irons. The Sulṭān had sent Amīr Kurt Bai, one of the leading Amīrs, who had been Governor of Cairo, to Ibn 'Othmān with presents worth about 10,000 dīnārs. He had also conferred on the military Ḳāḍī of Ibn 'Othmān and his minister Ḳarājā Pasha above mentioned a sumptuous robe of honour with a wide yalbaghāwi border, and gave them permission to return to their own country. It was an obvious error of judgment on the part of the Sulṭān al-Ghūrī to dismiss the emissaries of Ibn 'Othmān before the return of Moghul Bai with trustworthy news of Ibn 'Othmān.

[43] Kurt Bai heard on his arrival at 'Aintāb that Ibn 'Othmān had refused peace, and had arrested Moghul Bai and put him in irons. He had meant to hang him, but let him off at the intercession of some of his ministers. Ibn 'Othmān also meant to shave his victim's beard. He suffered indescribable insults at Ibn 'Othmān's hand. On learning this Kurt Bai returned to Aleppo and informed the Sulṭān of what Selīm Shāh Ibn 'Othmān had done to Amīr Moghul Bai. He also reported the arrival of the advanced guard of Ibn 'Othmān's army at 'Aintāb, and of their having captured the fortresses Malaṭiyyeh, Behsinā, Kerker, and others.

The announcement of this bad news by Kurt Bai disturbed the Sulṭān and people, and the whole army.

The Sulṭān decorated Amīr 'Abd al-Razzāḳ and invested him with the governorship of the district of the tribe of Du'l Ghādir. The Sulṭān then left Aleppo, accompanied by the Chief of Amīrs Khāir Bai with a very strong escort.

The Governor and Amīrs of Aleppo also left with their troops, and halted a day's march from the city.

The infantry with them amounted to five thousand; these troops received at that time a month's pay from the Sulṭān. These were followed by Chief Amīr Sī Bai, Deputy of Damascus, Tamrāz, Deputy of Tripoli, Ṭarā Bai, Deputy of Ṣafad, and the Deputies of Ḥomṣ and of Gazah. Their departure from Aleppo took place on the 17th of the month Rejeb.

A rumour had got about that Ibn 'Othmān was advancing from one direction and Ibn Sūwār from another. Then the Sulṭān gave orders for the Army to march from Aleppo and occupy Jīlān, in order to engage the rebel Ibn 'Othmān, saying that he himself and the Amīrs would shortly follow to take part in the battle, and that the issue would be in accordance with God's will.

This is an extract from a letter of the commander of the Faithful to his son Ya'ḳūb. The same letter gives prices at Aleppo; the price of barley was 27 niṣfs an ardebb; bread 3 dirhems a raṭl; cheese 2 niṣfs a raṭl; meat 9 dirhems a raṭl; Egyptian molasses half a feḍḍah a raṭl. The price of wheat went up as high as 2 ashrafīs an ardebb; and vetches (for camel-fodder) were selling at 124 dirhems the ardebb.

The Sulṭān issued an imperial edict to the Dawādār containing instructions as to his subjects. The imported Memlooks in quarters were not to molest the people or disturb the tradesmen. The Dawādār was to inquire into the cases of all those in the prisons, of both sexes, and to release debtors and others, in fact all except those imprisoned for a capital offence.

He also sent orders that if the road to the Ḥejāz were clear of Arabs, the pilgrimage to Mecca was to be started from Cairo, but that if the road was dangerous there was to be no pilgrimage that year. The imported Memlooks were to be forbidden to leave their quarters and enter the town, and anyone of them molesting the people was to be summarily dealt with and hung. These orders were read to them at the citadel in the presence of Amīr Ṭakṭ Bai, the Governor. The Sulṭān sent his greetings to all the Amīrs and troops.

The first day of the month of Sha'bān fell on a Friday; it was also the Coptic New Year's Day, which was regarded as an uncommon occurrence, especially as the latter was on a Friday, when there is a particular hour at which prayers are [44] answered. On the Saturday the Dawādār conferred a robe of honour on one of the Court, Jānī Bey al-Ḳaṣīr, a royal Memlook, and appointed him to the Inspectorship of Manfalūṭ in the place of Īnāl Ibn Jānī Bey, whose eyesight had failed.

On Sunday, the 3rd, the Dawādār inspected the prisoners in confinement and the women under arrest. He released a number of debtors, paying off their creditors himself. He also released a number of thieves, and ordered that a number of prisoners charged with murder should be cut in two. But he gave orders for the detention of some of the latter in prison till the Sulṭān's return. The Dawādār also gave substantial gifts to the poor. He commanded that the Khatmah should be read in all the mosques in Cairo, and that prayers should be offered up for the victory of the Sulṭān. On Monday, the 4th, he conferred a robe of honour on Yūsuf al-Badrī, and restored him to the position he formerly held in the Vizierate for the fourth time. On the same day orders were issued for the departure of the Ḥaj to Mecca as usual. It had been rumoured that there would be no pilgrimage this year.

On Tuesday or Tuesday night died the former Ḥanefī judge, Burhān al-Dīn Ibrāhīm Ibn al-Karakī, whose full name was Ibrāhīm Ibn al-Sheikh Zein al-Dīn 'Abd al-Raḥmān Ibn Ismā'īl al-Karakī al-Ḥanefī. He was a learned and distinguished man, an eminent chief of the Ḥanefī lawyers, a pupil of al-Sheikh Muḥyī al-Dīn al-Kāfījī, Sheikh Saif al-Dīn, and other learned Sheikhs of the Ḥanefī sect. He was Imām to al-Ashraf Ḳāit Bey, and rose to great distinction, holding many high posts, amongst which were Chief Sheikh of the College of the Sulṭān's mother in Tabbānah and accountant of the Sulṭān's household. After that he twice held the post of Chief Ḳāḍī of the Ḥanefīs. He then became head of the Ashrafiyyeh College, and endured much annoyance at the hands of Al-Ashraf. He had an agreeable countenance, was easy of approach, civil, and of a refined nature. He was in his eighth decade, he had lived a happy life, and died a witness to the faith; he had become very wealthy. The cause of his death was as follows: He was living at Birkah al-Fīl, and was going down to perform his ablutions at the Ḳaitūn steps, wearing a pair of clogs. He slipped and fell into the water; it was the Nile flood, and owing to the weight of his clothing he sank and was drowned.

On the same date the Dawādār conferred a robe of honour on one of the court officials named Ḳajmās, and appointed him to the Inspectorship of Menūfiyyeh in the place of Ḳānṣūh. News came from Aleppo of the death of Shems al-Dīn Muḥammed Ibn Nāshi, Sheikh of the Book-market, who was in close attendance on the Sulṭān. He had held a number of high offices. News also came of the death of Amīr Yūsuf, known as Maḳṭash, who had been Governor of Ṣafad; he was dismissed from that office and then died at Aleppo. The death of Abrak, one of the Amīrs of Tens and a former Inspector of the District of Gīzeh, was also reported.

A large number of those who were with the Sulṭān died of disease; and in Gazah, Damascus, and Aleppo many Amīrs of Tens, members of the Court, servants, and others died from disease incurred on the march. Confirmation of these reports was received during this month, and the news that the Sulṭān, when at Aleppo, promoted many Amīrs to the command of a thousand men. Amongst these were Amīr [45] Yūsuf al-Nāṣirī, superintendent of the buttery, Ṭarā Bai Ibn Yeshbek, Deputy of Ṣafad, Ḳānṣūh, Ustādār al-Ṣulḥbah, Ḳānṣūh al-Ashrafī, Deputy of the Citadel of Aleppo, Tamrāz, Deputy of Tripoli, and others. The Sulṭān, it appears, reduced many of the Chief Amīrs who were incapable, and promoted the above-named in their places.

On Friday, the 15th of Sha'bān, al-Ḥāj 'Alī al-Birmāwī died; he was Falconer and in charge of the Privy Purse. He rose to honours and greatness not hitherto reached by other Falconers, thanks to Dame Fortune. His death was caused by a pustule, which formed in his back; he was laid up for twelve days and then died. He was originally a fellāḥ of Birmah, and sold calico and carpets, riding on a donkey, till Providence opened a door for him. He never did anyone any harm, and was of a gentle and very humble disposition. After his death he was found to have been the possessor of five hundred thousand, six hundred dīnārs in gold, about forty-five brood mares and camels, one hundred head of buffalo, one thousand sheep, four hundred oxen at his irrigation wheels, and property of still greater value than what is enumerated above. The total amount of his property was valued at one hundred thousand dīnārs.

On Saturday, the 16th, came news of the great catastrophe which had overwhelmed the whole country. After a long absence of news of the Sulṭān and his army, a letter was brought by a runner alone from Amīr 'Allān Sub-Dawādār, one of the Chief Amīrs, telling that the Sulṭān believed and disbelieved by turns in Selīm Shāh Ibn 'Othmān, till finally Moghul Bey, Dawādār Sikkīn, arrived in a sorry plight wearing a mouldy cap without a tassel (?), an ancient dirty corslet (?) on his body, and riding on a wretched jade of a horse.

He had been deprived of his horses, baggage, and clothing. He brought the news that Ibn 'Othmān had refused to make peace, and had said to him: " Tell your master that he can meet us on Merj Dābeḳ." He also said that Ibn 'Othmān had put him in irons and wanted to shave off his beard, and had sent him to be hung on three occasions, but that some of his ministers had interceded for him. He had made him carry horse-dung in a basket on his head, and had subjected him to other insults and terrors.

When the Sulṭān heard this he realized the seriousness of the quarrel between himself and Ibn 'Othmān. It was said that the Sulṭān then gave Moghul Bey one thousand dīnārs, horses, and clothing to the extent of his losses.

Amongst other news of the Sulṭān it was commonly said by the people that he said the midday prayers, then mounted, and left the Aleppo Maidān on Tuesday, the 20th of Rejeb, accompanied by Amīr of the Faithful al-Mutewekkil 'alā Allāh, and the four judges. The Deputies of Damascus and Aleppo and a number of other deputies had started previously with an advance guard, preceded by drums, fifes, and gunners, so that Aleppo resounded with noise and excitement.

On the Sulṭān's departure from Aleppo he went to Ḥailan and halted there; on the morning of the 21st he left Jīlān and proceeded to Merj Dābeḳ, and remained there till the 25th. The latter was a day of constant ill fortune. He was suddenly surprised by the presence of a body of troops of Shāh Selīm Ibn 'Othmān. The Sulṭān said the morning prayers, mounted, and proceeded to Zaghzaghīn and Tell [46] al-Fār, where the alleged tomb of the Prophet Dā'ūd is. He there mounted his charger, wearing a light turban and a mantle, carrying an axe on his shoulder; he inspected the army in person; on the right wing was the Amīr of the Faithful, also wearing a light turban and mantle, carrying an axe on his shoulder like the Sulṭān, and having over his head the Khalīfah's banner. Around the Sulṭān, borne on the heads of a body of nobles, were forty copies of the Ḳor'ān in yellow silk cases; one of these copies was in the handwriting of Imām 'Othmān Ibn 'Affān. There were also round him a body of dervishes, among whom was the successor of Seyyid Aḥmed al-Bedawī (founder of the Ṣūfī sect), accompanied by banners. There were also the heads of the Ḳādiriyyeh sect with their green banners, the successor of Seyyidī Aḥmed al-Rīfā'ī with his banners, and Sheikh 'Afīf al-Dīn, attendant in the mosque of Seyyidah Nefīsah with black banners. Alongside of the Khalīfah was the youth Ḳāsim Bey Ibn Aḥmed Bey Ibn 'Othmān, of whom mention has already been made; according to some authorities he had over his head a yellow, according to others a red, silk flag. The Royal Red Standard was carried about 20 yards behind the Sulṭān, and under it marched the chiefs of the Memlooks, Sunbul al-'Othmānī, the four judges, and Amīr Tamr al-Zardkāsh, one of the principal Amīrs. On the right flank of the troops was Amīr Sī Bai, Deputy of Damascus, and on the left flank Khāir Bey, Deputy of Aleppo. According to some authorities the first to be engaged in the battle was Atābek Sūdūn al-'Ajemī, with Malik al-'Umarā Sī Bai, Deputy of Damascus, and the Ḳarānisah Memlooks, but not the imported Memlooks. These, accompanied by a number of Deputies, fought desperately and put to flight the troops of Ibn 'Othmān, inflicting terrible losses and capturing seven standards, the guns on the carriages, and the musketeers.

Ibn 'Othmān, in consequence, thought seriously of a retreat or a surrender, as over 10,000 of his men had been killed. At first the army of Egypt was victorious; would that it had continued so! But a report reached the Ḳarānisah Memlooks that the Sulṭān had ordered the imported Memlooks not to go into action at all, but to let the Ḳarānisah Memlooks fight alone, which damped their ardour. Meanwhile Atābek Sūdūn had fallen, also Malik al-'Umarā Sī Bai, Deputy of Damascus, and a great number of the right flank turned defeated. This was followed by the flight of Khāir Bey, Deputy of Aleppo, and the defeat of the left flank, Amīr Ḳānṣūh Ibn Sulṭān Chirkess being taken prisoner, some said killed. Moreover, Khāir Bey was said to be secretly in league with Ibn 'Othmān against al-Ghūrī, a report which was confirmed later. He was, moreover, the first to fly before all the troops, and proclaimed defeat. But this loss was inflicted on the Egyptian troops by the will of Providence in fulfilment of His decrees.

Now the Sulṭān was standing under the flag with a small body of Memlooks, and he began to call out: "Oh, sirs, now is the time to quit yourselves like men, this is the time to show your valour." But none listened to him, and they began to leave him, whilst he told the Faḳīrs to pray to God for victory, "for now," said he, "your prayers are needed." But no help or succour came. The Sulṭān's heart became as a red-hot coal, which could not be extinguished. The day, too, was fiercely hot, and such a dust was raised between the opposing armies that they could scarcely see each other. God's anger was kindled against the Egyptian troops, and their hands seemed to be fettered so that they could not fight, [47] and their sight failed them. I wrote these verses about the battle:—

When our Sulṭān with his army
Met the foe on the field of Merj Dābeḳ,
He cried, "Is there any to succour me?"
The tongue of events replied:
"Thou hast exposed thyself to calamity and thou must be the butt of it."
Terror struck the hearts of the foreign Memlooks,
So that they cried out "Where shall we hide?"
The sordidness of their minds so filled them with the lust for plunder,
That it brought about their destruction.

Now as the confusion and terror increased Amīr Tamr al-Zardkāsh feared for the safety of the Sulṭān's standard, so he lowered it, folded it up, and concealed it. Then he approached the Sulṭān and said to him: "Our King and Master, the troops of Ibn 'Othmān are upon us, save thyself and go back to Aleppo." When the Sulṭān understood this a kind of paralysis fell upon him, which affected one side, and caused his jaw to drop. He asked for water, and they brought him some in a golden cup, from which he drank a little. Then intending flight, he turned his horse round, moved on a few paces, fell off his horse, stood for a moment, and died from the shock of his defeat. It was said that his gall-bladder burst, and that red blood flowed from his throat.

When his death became known Ibn 'Othmān's troops advanced against the men who were round the Sulṭān; they killed Amīr Baibars, one of the Commanders, and a number of the bodyguard and of the Sulṭān's servants. As to the Sulṭān, his body was not found amongst the dead, nor was it ever known what became of it; it was as if the earth had swallowed it up there and then. Therein is a lesson to him who considers.

The Ottoman troops then trampled down al-Ghūrī's tents and overthrew all the goods and provisions stacked round them. The copy of 'Othmān's Ḳor'ān was lost, they stamped upon the Fakīrs' flags and the Amīrs' banners, and plundered everything belonging to the Egyptian troops.

Thus the rule of al-Ashraf al-Ghūrī came to an end, in the twinkling of an eye, as though he had never been. Praise be to Him whose kingdom never wanes, and Who never changes! Thus he and his kingdom came to an end together; the kingdom of Egypt and the Dominion of Syria, over which he had reigned for fifteen years nine months and twenty days. The date of his accession was the 1st of Shawwāl A.H. 906, and he died on the 25th of Rejeb, A.H. 922. During this period his subjects were in a miserable condition. Then I said:—

> Look with wonder at al-Ashraf al-Ghūrī,
> Who, after his tyranny had reached its height in Cairo,
> Lost his kingdom in an hour,
> Lost this world and the world to come.

This battle lasted from sunrise till the afternoon, and ended as God had decreed. The killed on both sides were innumerable. Three of the Chief Amīrs were killed, Atābek Ṣūdūn al-'Ajemī, Baibars, the kinsman (?) of the Sulṭān, and Aḳ Bai al-Ṭawīl. Ḳānṣūh Ibn Sulṭān Chirkess was taken prisoner. The following were also killed: Sī Bai, Deputy of Damascus; Tamrāz, Deputy of Tripoli; Ṭarā Bai, Deputy of Ṣafad; and Aṣlān, Deputy of Ḥomṣ; besides a great many Amīrs of Damascus, Aleppo, and Tripoli, a number of

[48] Egyptian Amīrs, Amīrs of the Ṭablkhānah, Amīrs of Tens and Guards.

Of the Egyptian troops, the Ḳarānisah Memlooks suffered the most, but few of the imported Memlooks were in action; no feats of horsemanship were displayed by them; in fact, they drew neither sword nor lance, and might have been blocks of wood for all the stir they made.

It was a time to turn an infant's hair white, and to melt iron in its fury. Merj Dābeḳ was strewn with corpses and headless bodies, and faces covered with dust and grown hideous. Dead horses lay everywhere, saddles were scattered about, also swords inlaid with gold, steel sets of horse-armour inlaid with gold, helmets, armour, and bundles of clothing. No one paid any heed to these things, for both armies were occupied with matters of more importance. A popular poem says:—

My horse beat applause when I had touched my lute on the
day of battle,
And sharp swords sang East and West;
They struck again and again, hitting in the music of the blows
The heads of the enemy—and dancing
As they entered into the fight.

Then Ibn 'Othmān advanced with his troops, and took possession of the Sulṭān's camp. He sat in the circular tent, took the wardrobe (?) and the costly goblets belonging to it, the armour-case, the weapons, the money-chest, and all articles of value, and each of his Amīrs took to himself a tent of one of al-Ghūrī's Amīrs. The troops occupied the tents of the Egyptian, Syrian, and Aleppo troops, thus exemplifying the maxim that "The misfortunes of some are the good fortunes of others". No Ottoman king has ever gained such a victory, but once Tīmūrleng entered Ibn 'Othmān's country, and fought against one of his ancestors, named Yildirim, who was defeated, taken prisoner, and placed by Tīmūrleng in an iron cage, and exposed to the ridicule of the people in Tīmūrleng's country. Being unable to bear it he swallowed a diamond ring and died in the cage.

No Sulṭān of Egypt ever suffered such a reverse in one day, or died under his standard, having all his property and equipment captured by the enemy, except Ḳānṣūh al-Ghūrī.

Thus was it written in the Divine decrees. Neither the Sulṭān nor his Amīrs ruled the people justly; they reaped the reward of their evil doings, and were vanquished by Ibn 'Othmān. Truly it has been said, "Where are the kings who wrought oppression in the land, and from whom God has freed the country?"

Then the Sulṭān Ibn 'Othmān left Merj Dābeḳ and entered Aleppo, taking possession of it without opposition; and he halted on the same Maidān that al-Ghūrī had previously [49] occupied. This is the full account of the battle as received by us, and all that passed between al-Ghūrī and Ibn 'Othmān.

The Amīrs and troops after their defeat made for Aleppo, but on trying to enter that town they were attacked by the inhabitants, who killed a number of the soldiers, taking their arms, horses, and equipment and laying hands on the things they had left in the town for security. Indeed, they suffered worse treatment at the hands of the people of Aleppo than they did from the soldiers of Ibn 'Othmān. There had been bad feeling between the people of Aleppo and the Imperial Memlooks since they had gone on ahead of the Sulṭān from Cairo to Aleppo, along with Ḳāṇī Bey, Grand Master of the Horse. They had forced an entrance into the houses of the people, violating their women and children; so the people of Aleppo had suffered much injury from them. No sooner did they realize that these troops were beaten, than they set about to take their revenge.

When the Amīrs and the remnant of the soldiers saw this they quitted Aleppo precipitately and made for Damascus, which they reached in the sorriest plight, deprived of clothing and horses. Most of the troops entered Damascus, some riding on donkeys, some on camels; many were almost naked, with just a cloak round them.

Never before had such a disaster befallen Egyptian troops.

The Amīrs, the executive officers, and the soldiers remained in Damascus until the survivors should arrive and it should be known who had died and who was still alive. It was said that the Amīrs when in Damascus had no protection from the burning sun, until their servants made them shelters from branches of trees. As to Selīm Shāh Ibn 'Othmān, he took up his quarters in the Maidān of Aleppo. Then Amīr al-Mu'minīn al-Mutewekkil 'alā Allāh approached him and the three chief judges, Kemāl al-Dīn al-Ṭawīl, Muḥyī al-Dīn al-Demīrī, Shihāb al-Dīn Futūḥi, of the Shāfi'i Māliki and Ḥanbalī sects respectively. Ḳāḍī Maḥmūd Ibn al-Shiḥnah had fled with the troops to Damascus, having been plundered of all his baggage and clothing. He arrived at Damascus in a miserable condition.

It was said that when the Amīr al-Mu'minīn presented himself to Ibn 'Othmān in the Maidān, the latter treated him with respect and asked him to be seated. He inquired where he came from, and on being told from Baghdād promised to send him back there ; but many different stories were circulated on the subject. When the Khalīfah requested leave to depart the Sulṭān presented him with a robe of honour from his own clothing, and gave him a sum of money and sent him back to Aleppo, putting him under observation so that he should not escape.

The story told about the three judges was that the Sulṭān abused them and said that they took bribes for their administration of the Sacred Law, and canvassed for offices by bribery ; that not one of them set an example of good conduct, for they did not prevent their Sulṭān from oppressing the people but looked on at this and did not condemn it. All kinds of strange stories were told and credited as true.

I was informed by one who saw Selīm Shāh Ibn 'Othmān that he was a square-built, broad-chested man, of a fair complexion, wide between the eyes, with an aquiline nose [perhaps a misprint for *Aḳna'l'Anf* (?)], a stout figure, with a moustache, but no beard, big-headed, wearing a small turban, smaller than those worn by his Amīrs. On his arrival at Aleppo, the people surrendered the town to him without opposition. Ḳānṣūh al-Ashraf, Governor of the Citadel, fled with the troops to Damascus, leaving the gates [50] of the Citadel open.

When this news reached Ibn ‘Othmān he sent off a man who was lame and beardless, with a wooden club in his hand, who went up to the citadel, entered it without opposition, affixed seals to the stores therein, and took possession of money, arms, and other articles of value. Ibn ‘Othmān did this that it might be said that he took the citadel of Aleppo by means of a lame man with a wooden club, and the weakest man in his army. Someone has said: "Take care not to despise a weak foe, for a fly can make the lion's eye bleed."

It was reported that Ibn ‘Othmān after capturing the town of Aleppo only entered it on three occasions. First when he went up to the citadel to inspect the stores, amongst which he found an amazing quantity of money, arms, and articles of value. The money amounted to about a million dīnārs. He also found gilt horsings and stirrups, axes and saddles inlaid with gold and crystal, side-drums, studded bridles, costly rings, sets of painted steel horse-armour, splendid helmets and other weapons, such as neither he nor any of his ancestors had ever seen or owned before, nor any of the Emperors of Constantinople. For what al-Ghūrī had collected by oppression and violence, and the valuables he had extracted from the treasuries of former kings of the Circassian Turks were quietly taken possession of by Selīm Ibn ‘Othmān without any trouble whatever. And not included in this was the property left in Ḥalab by the Amīrs in Command, the Amīrs of the Ṭablkhānah and the Amīrs of Tens, and the executive officers and soldiers, in the shape of money, arms, clothing, and equipment. It was also said that Ibn ‘Othmān took possession of thirteen citadels in the Sulṭān's dominions, and the property they contained. In fact, the quantity of money, arms, and valuables which he captured was unlimited. He became possessed of it all, by destiny. He also took innumerable horses, mules, camels, and tents. Bearing on which someone has said :—

> Does it not chance that one is deprived of his portion, though wide awake,
>
> While another obtains his, even while he sleeps.

The second occasion of Ibn 'Othmān's visit to the citadel was when he went to say the Friday prayers in the mosque of al-Ūṭrūsh, where his name was mentioned in them. Prayers were also offered up for him from the pulpits in the town of Aleppo and the surrounding districts. The town was illuminated, candles lighted in the bazaars, and voices were raised in prayer for him as he passed by on his return from the mosque, and the people made great rejoicings.

Ibrāhīm al-Samarḳāndī, Yūnus al-'Ādilī, and al-'Ajemī al-Shenḳjī declared themselves for him. These were close companions of al-Ghūrī, but had been secretly in league with Ibn 'Othmān, and in correspondence with him about the affairs of the Sulṭān and the country. When al-Ghūrī was gone, they showed the same friendship to Ibn 'Othmān, and set to work to depreciate al-Ghūrī and to enumerate his base actions to Ibn 'Othmān, becoming at last his adherents, and forgetting all al-Ghūrī's kindness to themselves.

[51] Another who had been secretly plotting against the Sulṭān was Khāir Bey, Governor of Aleppo. He was the first to cause the Sulṭān's troops to break, when he deserted the left flank, and went off in the direction of Ḥamāh. When Ibn 'Othmān had taken possession of Aleppo he sent for Khāir Bey and conferred a robe of honour upon him ; he became one of his Amīrs and took to wearing the round turban and black tassel of a Turkoman, and clipped his beard short. Thus he tendered his submission to Ibn 'Othmān, who called him Khāin Bey (traitor) because he betrayed his own Sulṭān.

When this took place his own Memlooks deserted him, and went off with the troops to Egypt. This event bears a close resemblance to the case of Ibn al-'Alḳamī, Vizīr of Baghdād, who plotted against the Khalīfah al-Musta'ṣim Bi'llāh. When Hūlāgū became Sulṭān of Baghdad, and killed the Khalīfah, he became a close attendant on Hūlāgū, who then turned against him and killed him, saying: "You were no good to your own master, and are not likely to be of any good to me." Very probably the same thing will happen to Khāir Bey.

The third occasion on which Ibn 'Othmān entered Aleppo was when he went in to the bath; and he then bestowed a considerable sum of money on the Mu'allim.

Now the Khalīfah and the three judges, the Shāfi'ī, the Mālikī, and Ḥanbalī, remained interned in Aleppo, not leaving the city without the Sulṭān's permission. There also remained there, after the defeat, many leading men, including Ḳāḍī 'Abd al-Kerīm Ibn al-Jī'ān, Secretary to the Imperial Treasuries, 'Abd al-Kerīm Ibn Fakhīrat, one of the Secretaries to the Memlooks, and 'Abd al-Kerīm Ibn al-Admī, Accountant of the Armoury, Re'īs Muḥammed Ibn al-Ḳaisūnī, Imām to al-Ghūrī, and a number of others whose names I do not remember. These persons remained behind in Aleppo after the defeat waiting for permission to leave.

When Ibn 'Othmān entered the town he proclaimed security to all, and announced that trade should be carried on as usual. He also ordered that all persons who had horses, arms, or clothing belonging to the Amīrs or the troops were to bring them in to him, and that anyone failing to do this, if denounced, was to be hung forthwith.

[Here follows a list of Amīrs and others killed in the battle, or made prisoners, omitted in the translation.]

* * * * *

[52] Now let us return to what was taking place in Cairo. On the arrival of the letter from Amīr 'Allān, the Sub-Dawādār, giving an account of the terrible battle, and of the loss of the Amīrs, nobles, and judges, there arose great lamentations in the family of Atābek Sūdūn al-'Ajemī, for he

was a devout, good, and kind-hearted Amīr. He was known as Sūdūn Ibn Jānī Bey, and was originally one of Ashraf Ḳāit Bey's Memlooks. He had held several high offices, including that of Amīr Mejlis and Chief Armour-bearer. He showed great courage in action, and splendid feats of horsemanship; he continued to a fight till he was killed on his horse. May the Lord have mercy on him. So there was mourning for the Sulṭān that day, and for the Amīrs and nobles, and lamentation and weeping in all the thoroughfares of Cairo, for [53] those who had fallen. Cairo and its people were in great agitation, confusion, and wild talk reigned everywhere.

On Sunday, the 17th Sha'bān, the Dawādār heard that the Beni 'Aṭiyyeh and Na'ā'im Arabs had plundered the estates of the Sharḳīeh province and carried off about 400 head of sheep belonging to the Sulṭān, and had gone into the Wādī 'Abbāsah. On hearing this the Dawādār performed the midday prayers, and then rode out with five hundred Memlooks to meet the Arabs, came upon them suddenly, and they fled from before him, and the Amīr and his party recovered all the goods and sheep and crops and returned to Cairo the same day.

During this month he conferred a robe of honour on Zeinī Berekāt Ibn Mūsā. He also went about Cairo issuing proclamations to restore public confidence, and to abolish the system of exactions known as monthly and weekly payments and all recent oppressive measures. He declared that Zeinī Berekāt Ibn Mūsā would continue in office and that no one was to invoke the protection of anyone against him. So the Dawādār's influence and the esteem felt for him became twice as great as before.

He combined many high offices, and was supreme over the affairs of the country.

On Monday, the 18th, the Dawādār paid the troops in Cairo their wages. They were distributed by Amīr Ṭaḳṭ Bai, Deputy of the Citadel, at the steps. This was the occasion for much talk about the Sulṭān's death, and manifestations of distress thereat. On the same day the Dawādār ordered a parade of those in prison, including the women; and thereupon he set a large number at liberty, including Jān Bey, Dawādār of Amīr Ṭarā Bai, who had been in prison at Maḳsharah for some time, on account of money which he had embezzled whilst he was pleader in charge of the Sulṭān's Privy Purse. He also released Ḳāḍī Bedr al-Dīn Ibn Tha'lab, Ḳāḍī of Asyūṭ, who had also been imprisoned at Maḳsharah for arrears of fines. He further released his son Shems al-Dīn and his brother Nejm al-Dīn, together with Ṣalāḥ al-Dīn Ibn Kātib Gharīb, the nephew of Abū al-Faḍl, also the Mu'allim, Shenshū al-Yahūdī, a convert to Muḥammedanism, whose imprisonment has already been mentioned. He also set at liberty the Mu'allim Ya'ḳūb, the goldsmith, Mu'allim at the Mint, and a large number of workmen, fellaḥīn, and others, including the women who were in seclusion and nobles who were in prison, leaving in there only criminals and those charged with capital offences. He cut off the hands of a large number of the latter and let them go. He then cut in two a number of criminals, amongst whom was a man named 'Abd al-Ḳādir abū Diyat, and cut off the hands of several thieves. He discharged Ḳāḍī Ṣalāḥ al-Dīn Ibn Abī al-Su'ūd Ibn Ḳāḍī Ibrāhīm Ibn Ẓahīrah, Ḳāḍī of Mecca, who had been for some time in irons, in Zeinī Berekāt Ibn Mūsā's house. The circumstances that led to his arrest were the following. A certain Ibrāhīm al-Samarḳandī preferred a complaint against him to the Sulṭān that he had found a quantity of hidden treasure at Mecca. The Sulṭān then summoned the Ḳāḍī from Mecca in disgrace; on his arrival the Sulṭān demanded the treasure from him. He denied the existence of it, and the Sulṭān put him in irons in charge of Zeinī Berekāt, and he remained thus in his keeping for a long time though quite innocent.

[54] On Tuesday, the 19th, the Dawādār conferred a robe of honour on Shihābī Aḥmed Ibn al-Mundhirī Ḥasan Ibn al-Ṭūlūnī and restored him to the post of chief

Mu'allim, from which the Sulṭān had deposed him in favour of Jemāl al-Dīn al-Alwāḥī, guardian of Dahīshah. On the same day the Dawādār made proclamation in Cairo that all the recent taxes were abolished, and that the decrees in force under Ashraf Ḳāit Bey were to be observed. This was received with general acclamation. Zeinī Berekāt Ibn Mūsā went throughout Cairo fixing the prices of commodities, so that a kind of vermicelli, which was being sold at four dirhems the raṭl, was fixed at two dirhems ; cheese and meat also came under the new tariff.

During the same month Zeinī opened the dam at Abū Manja, the Nile having risen on that day to twenty cubits. This was on the 22nd day of Tūt, the first Coptic month. The Dawādār used during the Sulṭān's absence to ride out to Maṭariyyeh daily, and on his return to enter by the Bāb al-Naṣr, preceded by the Chief Amīrs who had remained behind in Egypt, and a strong body of troops. Immediately in front of him were runners and naptha throwers (?), and his Memlooks wearing swords and carrying lances with coloured silk pennons.

These processions caused a great sensation in Cairo, and the people received him with shouts of welcome. He used to picture himself as Sulṭān before he became so ; he had, in fact, become very powerful and was greatly feared.

On Friday, the 22nd, when the Sulṭān's death was confirmed, the preachers did not offer up prayers for the Sulṭān, nor was his name mentioned from the pulpits, but only the Khalīfah's ; and some said, " May God appoint our best over us, and not our worst."

This state of affairs went on for a long time, Egypt remaining without a Sulṭān, and likewise the dominions of Syria. During this time the Arabs committed depredations in the eastern and other districts. They plundered a number of dwellings, carrying off all the cattle and sheep, and even robbing the women of their jewellery. An enormous number of Fellāḥīn were killed during these troubles besides messengers and others; the roads were closed to travellers, affairs grew even worse when the Sulṭān's death became certainly known, and confusion reigned in Egypt. All kinds of ill-omened reports were spread as to the fate of the Sulṭān and his army.

The most notorious in these depredations were the followers and a number of the 'Ashīr of the Arab Sheikh Amīr Ahmed Ibn Baḳar. They committed excesses, specially amongst the soldiers and merchants, who came in with the caravans from Syria; they killed great numbers of them, stealing their property and camels. Those who escaped death were stripped bare. In fact, the troops suffered worse things at the hands of these Arabs than they did from Ibn 'Othmān; and this after they had reached safety, between Ḳatīyā and Ṣāliḥiyyeh.

It was also rumoured that the imported Memlooks had planned to come down from the barracks to loot and burn Ḳhān al-Khalīlī and kill the Turkish merchants there, for they said, "These merchants are on the side of Ibn 'Othmān, and exulted in the death of our master."

When the Dawādār heard of this he summoned the officers
[55] in charge and said to them, "I look to you alone to prevent this sedition," and forbade them to leave the barracks. Had it not been for the timely intervention of the Dawādār, who smothered the smouldering insurrection, Cairo would have been completely wrecked by the imported Memlooks.

During the same month the Dawādār gave his attention to the manufacture of certain weapons of war, such as wooden shields and muskets and other things of this nature. It was reported that he would become Sulṭān before the return of the army. The mover in this matter was Amīr Ṭaḳṭ Bai, Governor of the Citadel, and Amīr 'Allān, second Dawādār. As on the previous Friday the preachers did not mention the Sulṭān's name in the prayers.

After Amīr 'Allān's letter giving an account of the defeat of the army and of the Sulṭān's fate, there was an entire absence of any authentic news for about forty days. All kinds of rumours were afloat, one to the effect that Jān Birdī al-Ghazāli, Governor of Damascus, had stopped any going to Egypt and had detained the army in Damascus.

News also arrived from Amīr Ḥusein, Deputy of Jeddah, and al-Re'īs Selmān al-'Othmānī, that on proceeding on the way to Hind (along the Arabian coast) with the army before mentioned and arriving at Kamrān (near Zabīd, in Yemen), a Hind village, they built a fortress with flanking towers, completing it in about five months. Amīr Ḥusein then dispatched a body of troops towards a place called al-Liḥyah, and another to Mūrā, whilst he himself with the rest of the army remained at Beit al-Fityah for about a month. After that Amīr Ḥusein and Re'īs Selmān proceeded with their troops against Zabīd, in the possession of 'Abd al-Malik, brother of Sheikh 'Āmir.

This he besieged, and captured it on Friday morning, the 20th of Jumādā al-Ākhirah, A.H. 922. They found a large population there. The same letter also announced that Ḥusein, after taking Zabīd, attacked the fortress of the town of Aden, and nearly took it. Also that they had appointed to the command of Zabīd one of Ashraf al-Ghūrī's Memlooks, one of the Amīrs of Tens named Bars Bai. The latter had with him some Memlooks and followers, being joined also by a body of about 10,000 Arabs. So when Bars Bai became possessed of Zabīd he governed the place like a Sulṭān, and appointed a Dawādār, a treasurer, and officials as Sulṭān's do. He and his troops acquired great spoils there.

During this month also the Dawādār inspected the troops in Cairo. The inspection took place from his house. He thought this necessary because he had intelligence that a number of ships had been sighted outside the frontier towns of Alexandria and Rashīd ; and he was afraid they might have been sent by Ibn 'Othman. So he lost no time in parading the soldiers and telling them to be on the alert, and to get their kit (?) ready in case this news should be confirmed. Then the meeting broke up and the soldiers went off in frantic haste.

On Saturday, the first day of Ramaḍān, many of the Deputy Judges called on the Dawādār and congratulated him on the new month. The three Chief Judges and the Khalīfah, being prisoners of Selīm Shāh Ibn 'Othmān at Aleppo, were [56] unable to return to Egypt. On Sunday, the 12th day of Ramaḍān, corresponding to the 1st of the Coptic month Bābah, the Nile remained steady at 20 cubits; it had risen higher in the previous year, and continued unabated until the 1st of Hātūr.

Then came the news by a messenger [already related in pp. 46, 47] of the miserable condition of the troops who reached Damascus, of the treachery of al-Ghūrī's former friends, and that Ibn 'Othmān was sole master from the Euphrates to Aleppo. When the Dawādār heard of this he ordered the Vālī to take possession of the houses belonging to Samarḳandi and Yūnus al-'Ādilī. So the Vālī went there and arrested their families and retainers, placed Samarḳandī's servant in irons, and put seals on his stores and on those of Yūnus al-'Ādilī. They had been in secret correspondence with Selīm Shāh Ibn 'Othmān, about the affairs of the Sulṭān and the country. But the master of the house has the best knowledge of what goes on in it.

On Friday, the 17th, the Dawādār said the Friday prayers, and then went on to meet the Chief Amīrs, who were arriving from Damascus; he had heard of their reaching Belbeis. [The list of names is here omitted.]

* * * * *

The remnant of the army came, in the most pitiful state of nakedness, hunger, and weakness, with their garments opened at the neck, and manifested their grief about the Sulṭān.

Thus the Amīrs and the army made their way in. [Another list of names is omitted.]

* * * * *

Thursday, the 13th, witnessed the arrival of all the Amīrs that were left. After greeting them the Dawādār returned

[57] home, and with them came Amīr Ḳānṣūh al-Ashrafī, who was in charge of the fortress at Aleppo. He it was who surrendered it with all it contained (see p. 48), although the citadel of Aleppo was strongly fortified. Therefore, when the Dawādār confronted him he severely reproved him, ordered his imprisonment in the citadel-tower, and threatened him with severe punishment.

Now on the return of the Amīrs to Cairo, they were unanimous for the election of Ṭūmān Bai, the Dawādār, as Sulṭān.

But he persisted in his refusal; the Amīrs replied that there was no one else but him, and that there was no way out of it, whether he wished it or not. Then the Dawādār mounted his horse and accompanied by a number of the leading Amīrs [list of names omitted] proceeded to Sheikh Abū Su'ūd, who was at Kaum al-Jāriḥ. When they were all seated they explained the matter to him—of their desire that the Dawādār should be Sulṭān and of the Dawādār's refusal. Then the Sheikh produced a Ḳor'ān and made the Amīrs swear on it that if they made him Sulṭān they would not betray him nor intrigue against him, but would cheerfully accept what he said and did. And they all swore to this. The Sheikh made them also swear that they would not go back to their old oppression of the people, nor proceed against any except as laid down by law; that they would abolish the tyrannical innovations of al-Ghūrī, including the impositions on the shops, and carry on affairs as in the day of al-Ashraf Ḳāit Bai, and conduct the Ḥisbah as did Yeshbek al-Jemālī when he was Censor. Then they swore to all this, and the Sheikh told them that Allah had brought all these disasters and humiliations and Ibn 'Othmān's victory only in response to the curses of the people upon them both on sea and land. To which they replied that they repented before Allah from that day forth for their acts of oppression.

Then the meeting broke up and they left; the Sheikh Abū Su'ūd agreed to appoint the Dawādār as Sulṭān. The Dawādār accepted their compact, confirmed by oath in his presence, and became Sulṭān.

The accession of the Dawādār to the Sulṭānate took place as will be described.

[58] At this point we will return to Ashraf al-Ghūrī. [The story of al-Ghūrī's advance against Ibn 'Othmān, his first success and subsequent defeat in the battle of Merj Dābeḳ, of the Sūlṭān's death, and the disappearance of his body is here repeated, which have been already told in greater detail in pp. 41–4.]

* * * * *

It was extraordinary that al-Ghūrī was not buried at the College on which he had spent some 100,000 dīnārs, thinking that he would be buried in a fine tomb, but it was destined to be otherwise, and he lay stretched out on the waste, the prey of wolves and leopards. He died at about the age of 78, having reigned over Egypt and Syria for 15 years 9 months 25 days, every day of which seemed to the people a thousand years.

As to his appearance, he was tall, bulky, big-bellied, fair-complexioned, round-faced, sleek-eyed, and loud-voiced; with a circular beard scarcely showing any white hair in it. He was looked up to with awe as a king, satisfying the eyes of all beholders with the magnificence of his pageants. Had it not been for his tyranny and exactions, he would have been one of the best of the Circassian Sulṭāns; and, indeed, one of the best of all the Sulṭāns of Egypt. On Mondays and Thursdays he used to go down to the Royal Enclosures (for game), and on Saturdays and Tuesdays to the Maidān. He used to go down by Sab' Ḥadrāt, preceded by a pair of horses with gold saddles and gold-embroidered saddle-cloths, and he would often make riding expeditions on Bedouin saddles and broad stirrups, and he used to fasten a golden girth round his waist instead of the Ba'lbec waist-band. He used to wear rings of ruby, turquoise, emerald, diamond, and cats' eyes, and he was addicted to smelling sweet scents, such as musk, aloes, and amber. He was fastidious in his dress, fond of flowers, fruit, and other dainties. He probably inclined to the Nesīmiyyeh views from his liking for associating with foreigners. He was fond of planting trees and of gardens, and of listening to singing birds, and of smelling fragrant flowers. He drank out of gold cups, was fond of pleasures, eating and drinking greedily. He was known as Ḳānṣūh Ibn Bībardi al-Ghūrī. He lived constantly in this luxurious way in the kingdom of Egypt, obeyed and feared by all, keeping a tight hold over the Amīrs and Nawābs and the soldiers. He was unthwarted until he and Selīm Shāh Ibn 'Othmān, Emperor of Constantinople, quarrelled, and he went out, as I have [59] related, to meet him, and such a tragedy happened as never happened to any other King of Egypt or elsewhere.

I have perused the history of kings,
And have not heard the like of such events;
Time never ceases to work wonders and strange things amongst men,
But such an event has never before happened to Sulṭān or ruler.
Al-Ashraf al-Ghūrī was our king.
But he practised tyranny and calumny amongst us,
Death rendered inevitable his defeat with his army,
That was written in the Divine Decrees;
His deeds have recoiled on himself,
And time has brought the retribution of Fate.

Amongst the Sulṭān's virtues it may be said that he was good-natured, controlled his temper, and considering his strong passions was not over-violent. He had a great belief in the dervishes and the pious, was a good judge of a man's capacities, and was not vituperative in fits of anger.

He understood poetry, and was fond of instrumental music and singing. He was not excitable. He was very fond of reading history and travels, and collections of poetry. He was affable, liking joking and jesting in his company; though rough-looking he was amiable and civil by nature—contrary to the Turkish character. He had no haughtiness or self-glorification in him, nor the extreme effrontery shown by former kings in their doings.

When Jemāl al-Dīn was hanged, the Sulṭān appointed Mu'allim Ya'ḳūb, the Jew, to the Treasury. The latter acted as Jemāl al-Dīn had done. He considered himself entitled to do as he liked with the property of individual Muḥammedans. In a single night the good silver niṣf turned into mere red copper. Adulteration of the coinage went on all through the Sulṭān's reign, up to his death. There is an axiom in the sacred tradition : " He who deceives us is not of us."

[60] Amongst the evil practices he used to appoint the inspectors and Arab Sheikhs over fief-lands and pious foundations, and these would take many times their due. From this period the affairs of the country steadily deteriorated. Damascus and Aleppo also declined ; he used to make them liable for large sums every year, and they in turn would wring the money from their peasant subjects. So the owners of fiefs and settlements were anxious to leave their country for another, such was the oppression they suffered from their governors, more especially the Arabs of Jebel Nābulus, on account of the contributions that had been laid upon them for the infantry at the time of the expedition. The result was anything but good to the Syrian population.

Ḥusein, Deputy of Jeddah, used to lay a tax of ten per cent on the goods of Indian merchants, so they gave up coming into the port of Jeddah, and its prosperity declined. There was a scarcity of cotton-stuffs in Egypt, and also of goods imported from Europe, of rice and of leather ; the ports of Alexandria and Damietta similarly declined ; European merchants refusing to enter them owing to the extortions practised there. He placed an impost on the sale of corn, three niṣfs being taken on every ardebb from the seller and buyer, and an equal amount on melons and pomegranates.

He even put an embargo on salt. He renewed many taxes of such a kind as were not even imposed by Huniades in his time. No important trader escaped this system of extortion. He laid contributions on the Amīr of the Faithful al-Mu'minīn al-Mustemsik Bi'llāh Ya'ḳūb, and took a considerable sum of money from him. He incurred many debts, which led to his devising these schemes so as to pay the sum demanded of him. Many Amīrs died under his persecution, and several officials were imprisoned until death.

* * * * *

Amongst other wicked acts of the Sulṭān's was the expulsion of the *Aulād al-Nās* from their landsand employments without due cause, putting imported Memlooks in their places. He suspended the payments to infirm people, orphans of both sexes, and children, which caused them grievous privations. He removed the marble which was in the court of Yūsuf, Inspector of the Sulṭān's private domains, known as the Niṣf al-Dunyā, and put it in the Court of the Baisariyyeh in the citadel. He deprived the people of what they had been in the habit of receiving from the privy purse from time immemorial. He re-established the system of taxing the fief-holders before the rise of the Nile and the sowing of the land, subjecting them to insults and reducing them to misery. His avarice increased to such an extent that he wrung from the small cultivators a share of the profits they made from the cow-dung collected out of the gutters in the Maidān, making them pay it into the imperial coffers. Every functionary and employé suffered hardship from his daily extortions.

After the death of Amīr Khāir Bey, the treasurer, the Sulṭān took to managing the Treasury himself. He used to spend some of the large sums of money he obtained, on buildings [61]which were of no benefit to his subjects, on the decoration of walls, and the gilding of ceilings. This was a sheer waste of the public money. He would run away from trials at law, as a child runs away from school. None of the trials with which he was concerned were conducted in a decent fashion, but under repulsive conditions. He used to pay no attention to cases of murder, but would hand them over to the sacred tribunal, and the rights of the people in this respect were disregarded.

He was very negligent about signing edicts, few, in fact, received his signature, and business suffered in consequence. This led to the purchase of old stamps for an Ashrafi, that they might be affixed to edicts for the transaction of business. To describe all his faults in detail would occupy far too much space.

[Then follow the names of the Khalīfah and the Judges, the secretaries, etc., here omitted.]

* * * * *

[62] Among the buildings which the Sulṭān erected in Cairo the following may be mentioned :—

The Mosque and the College, which he built at Sharābishīyīn (i.e. the market of the makers of robes of honour, etc.), the depot, stores, and quarters behind the college, near the dye-works, and the double-pinnacled minaret which he added to the Mosque al-Azhar. He also built the quarters there, and the shops in the markets behind the Mosque, and the dwelling-places at Khān al-Khalīlī. He restored the building of Khān al-Khalīlī, and erected stores and shops there. He built two dwelling-houses and two shops at Bāb al-Ḳanṭarah, and two dwelling-houses between the two walls and the mill near the dye-works. He also built and highly decorated a house for his son at Bunduḳāniyīn, and erected a dwelling-quarter and an inn there. He made the Maidān below the citadel, and planted trees there brought from Syria, and arranged a supply of water by channels from the Nile. On this spot he constructed the belvederes and lake, the hall of justice, and the night-shelter. He also built a Mosque behind the Maidān and the Arab quarter, with a pulpit and a minaret. He restored the citadel building, including the Dahīshah and Baisariyyeh Hall, and the Hall of Columns, and the Hall of the Fish-pond (?). He built the Coptic resting-place at al-Ḥoush, and restored the kitchen at the citadel and the Fountain of the Faithful, giving a vaulted roof of masonry.

He also built the quarters and stores at the little market of 'Abd al-Mun'im, the quarters and the depot at the great bridge, and restored the buildings at Maidān Mahārah, near the Ḳanāṭir al-Sibā', building it of the famous bezil-stone, it being formerly of brick. He also constructed an aqueduct, bringing the water from the Derb al-Khaulī to the Mauridat al-Halfā, restored the Nilometer, and at the same place he built the palace and the seats overlooking the river. He restored the Ḳanṭarah Benī Wā'il, the Ḳanṭarah Jedīdah, the Ḳanṭarah al-Ḥājib, and the Ḳanṭarah al-Kharnūbī, making them high enough for ships to pass through. He also restored the bridge of lions. He built the Maṣṭabahs (seats ?), and placed over them the pillars near the cupola of Amīr Yeshbek at Maṭariyyeh. He erected on the shore of the Salt Lake a handsome citadel with towers, and a mosque with a pulpit; and he built on to the fortress at Rashīd a wall and watch-towers to protect it. He restored the towers at Alexandria, repaired the 'Aḳabah road and the stone circle [1] and built a caravanserai there, with towers at the gate. [63] He also made storehouses there for the property of the pilgrims. He built a caravanserai in Azlem, with warehouses in it, like the one in 'Aḳabah. He also dug wells in various watering-places of the pilgrims.

At Mecca he built a college with a hostel for the students and hermits there; he also renewed the water-supply at Bāzān, which had been cut off for some years. At Jeddah he erected a sea-wall with several towers, to protect the port against the Franks; this wall was one of the best buildings there. Many other good buildings which were of service to the Muḥammedans were erected under his auspices.

To sum up, it may be said that the Sulṭān al-Ghūrī was the best of the Circassian Sulṭāns, notwithstanding some crooked

[1] These "consist of huge stone circles, some of them measuring 100 feet in diameter, having a cist in the centre covered with a heap of large boulders. These are nearly identical in construction with the Druidical circles of Britain" (Palmer's *Desert of the Exodus*, pt. i, p. 140, Cambridge, 1871).

ways. No succeeding king acted like him, or possessed his soaring ambition and determination. He had the qualifications of an emperor, and was a striking figure in royal pageants. And there is no harm in quoting this "zajal" composed by Sheikh Bedr al-Dīn, may God preserve him, in lamentation over al-Malik, al-Ashraf, Ḳanṣūh al-Ghūri on the occasion of the revolution aforementioned and what befel him.

* * * * *

[64] The sun of the empire of al-Ghūrī has set,
And the star of Ibn 'Othmān has risen.
This is the decree of the Lord of Heaven,
And the world turns round for ever.
Ibn 'Othmān showed open hostility to him by taking the citadel,
And by preventing both the merchants and slave-dealers from bringing Memlooks into Egypt,
Or furs or sables, squirrels and foxes.
We have no more woollen clothes; oh, the years we have waited for wool!
But no merchant brings any.
The Amīrs came to the king and said
"Ibn 'Othmān is rebelling against you."
The great Amīr was called Sūdūn,
He bore the unusual surname of al-'Ajemī;
And the exalted Maḳarr Ashrafī the Amīr of Arms, named Erkmās,
And the chief of the guards named Sūdūn,
He is as much trained as the other races.
Anas Bai was the chief chamberlain, brave in battle, a fine swordsman;
Muḥammed, called Chief Master of the Horse, was a son of the Sulṭān,
Most noble, valued, victorious;
The Sub-Dawādār was Amīr 'Allān; and if you would hear of the Chief Amīrs,
They were: Ibn Chirkess, a great leader, and Tamr, known as the Armourer;
Jān Balāṭ and Kurt Bai, some forty others, and more,

Bands heralding victory, mounted men in large number, and 'Asharawāts of Turks.

These all held council together, and said :

" Our hearts and spirits are weary, but we are all going out to battle,

With led horses, arms, and accoutrements ;

We unsheathe the sword to win victory for the Sulṭān,

We shall defeat the Turk and tread down his country."

Like gamblers they wagered their lives, each one casting with it,

Not knowing what all-conquering fate has in store for him.

The 15th of Rebi' al-Ākhir, 922 (dated from the Flight of the Guide and Intercessor for mankind

On the Resurrection Day) was the date of the Sulṭān's departure

On the expedition against Ibn 'Othmān, intent on conquering the dominion of Syria.

[65] The Amīrs were arrayed in his service,

Vying with one another in the splendour of their retinue,

With their splendid Memlooks and battalions.

The departure from Cairo was under the decree of the Almighty;

The Sulṭān was accompanied by his chosen secretary, Ḳāḍī Maḥmūd, in a litter

With the chief judges and their deputies, each doing his best,

And the Khalīfah, al-Mutewekkil, son of Ya'kūb Muḥammed,

Whose good deeds are commended ;

With him also went his Chief Minister, with a view to the robes of honour,

The mouthpiece of his yea and nay ;

Al-Ḳaṣrawī was his chief executive officer and Commander-in-chief of his army.

They entered Syria with a cavalcade the like of which had never before been heard of nor seen ;

Nor king, nor Sulṭān, nor any other had been attended by such a concourse.

From Damascus, Aleppo was entered, and its rugged and smooth places traversed.

Selīm Shāh, hearing thereof, showed that his nature was struck with amazement.

He sued for peace, sending an envoy with gifts and costly garments.

They said: "Peace is in the hands of the Lord of Decrees,
Whosoever opposeth him turneth right guidance into error;
Man is the bearer of the trust committed to him,
The lofty mountains refuse to carry it."
Our Lord ordained the sparing of blood,
And saved the believers the trouble of fighting.
The spies of al-Ashraf al-Ghūrī returned;
They informed him of a plot against him.
They said: "Beware of trusting to Ibn 'Othmān's peace,
And know that he is treacherous towards you."
He believed their words, and started for Aleppo with his hosts for battle;
He found the Turks [Rūm] fully armed, and the quivers equipped with arrows.
Such a struggle took place between the armies as would have turned the hair of children white to hear of;
Allah gave the Egyptians victory over the Turks.
Their cavalry was seen at noon bearing down upon them.
Man knows not what is laid up for him,
Nor towards what destiny he is moving;
Ibn 'Othmān had troops lying in ambush on his left,
Whilst our men were busy plundering the Turks,
They attacked on our right flank, and the Sulṭān gave a cry for help.
And there were robbers by him.
He was thrown from his horse, and lay moaning;
His cousin Bībars and Aḳ Bai Ṭawīl hurried up to his aid,
But courage cannot avail against numbers;
They cut them up with the sharp sword.
Glory to the Lord of all movement!
Allāh makes a cause for the death of each.
Al-Ghūrī's defeat was a great surprise, written in history with letters of gold.
What happened to him took place on the 2nd of Rejeb of the year A.H. 922.
[66] I ask God to brighten the future, and that He should make the gainer into the loser once more;
That it may please him to remove shame from us by giving revenge,
By bringing defeat on the head of the infidel;

I desire revenge for the death of al-Ghūrī, maybe I shall attain
my wishes;
Joy will be mine on that day, and they will sing to the string
or the Ṭar;
Then I shall not fear the bird of ill-omen, if it croaks in our
house or flies over it.
Al-Ghūrī's end was a strange thing, he went stalking with his
foot to his death;
We had taken all things into account, but that which befell
him did not cross our minds.
I weep for al-Ghūrī, a well of blood flows for my grief;
I long for eyes from the people [to help in my weeping];
From early morning till the sun set.
During the time of his reign happiness kept watch over him
till the evil eye struck him;
The steed disappeared amongst the enemy, it threw him, he
died, tears flowing from his eyes.
All who were jealous for him were glad when he had set out
against the raider.
I have likened this army to a garden,
In which the flowers on the branches are the horsemen,
The skirt on the coat of mail is the zephyr on the river,
And lo, he [=Ghūrī] appears like a drawn sword.
The vestment over the armour was as a full-blown red rose
amongst gardens;
The bunting was like gilt branches of willow guarded by sword-
poles [i.e. swords in lieu of poles];
The wounded bodies were like the jasmine, encircled by red
poppies.
In the sky of the battle appeared horsemen like stars adorning
their uniform;
The spear-points were like shooting-stars, and their helmets
like stars on suns.
The Sultān was like the eclipsed moon amongst them, their
strokes on the shields were like thunder.
Methought arrows were being launched from the rainbow at
the armies in a dust-storm like night;
The sky raining penetrating darts on the enemy and incessant
rain.

These soldiers were like garden-fruits, their blood the spilt juice of the grape ;
This one yellow as the colour of the apricot, another like the colour of the Jujube, another like that of a helmet.
No one has ever seen such an engagement as this one ;
Do not speak to me of Nāṣir, nor of Barḳūḳ.
The Amīrs resemble fruitful trees in the gardens, diffusing the most exquisite perfume ;
The guns hurled large quinces, or pomegranates, and remind one (?) of the proud stallions (?).
How much do I try to console my heart, and say to it, " Heart, reflect,"
Where is Suleimān, where Nimrod, where Pharaoh, and where Cæsar ?
[67] Where are the kings of other times, and he with the two horns, called Alexander ?
Where Chosroes Naushirwān and his pavilion ?
He is dead, and his palace (i.e. at Ctesiphon) remains deserted ;
Everything passes on by the decree of the Ancient of Days,
It is only the first and last who abides.
Were but a porter of this town to bet on a game, and lose,
We of his kindred would be sorry for his defeat ;
What, then, say you to the Sulṭān al-Ghūrī, being stripped and killed and dying in distress ?
Fifteen years nine months and twenty-five days it was exactly from the beginning of his reign.
A marvel there was in the death of Ghūrī, nothing fated can be averted by caution ;
The day he rode out with the cavalcade he knew not what was written on his forehead ;
The tongue of circumstance told him that there remained of his life three months.
Awake from the sleep of carelessness, shorten the length of hope ;
Nine days of the month must pass, and on the tenth comes thy destiny.
The Sulṭān was a chief courageous, the rear of Ibn 'Othmān's army seemed to be wrecked ;

The wind blew and loosened his boat, Ibn 'Othmān was floated off, and his victory was manifest;
The ships were sunk, and the sailors, with his sword he drove them all into the sea.
Their bodies and their blood made their sea into a land crowded with corpses;
And when he sailed away their land was as a sea flowing with blood.
The Creator, our Lord, the Lord of Glory, had unveiled for him the bride of the beauty of his kingdom,
But hid from him that he would fall dead from his horse on the day of battle;
It was concealed from him that he would die defeated,
And that his place of burial would never be known.
How many an augury he drew from the sand and the saint-augurs, God's augury is the most potent;
So all that he was depending on blew away, and this no bird had ever revealed to him.
I begin and end my verse by praising the Chosen One;
The lizard and the shoulder of mutton and the camel spoke to him;[1]
The trees hastened to his service, and the gazelle, whose tradition is well known;
The stones in the palm of his hand spake to him;
The moon was slit in two for him, after it had reached its full size and brightness;
He satisfied his army with (a little ?) food, and the water flowed gushing from his finger.
If they say Abū al-Nejā al-'Aufī is unequalled in the city for his poetry,
[68] O thou who comest to hear the pearls of his verses,
Take and write down the wonders of his chronicle;

[1] For these miracles *vide* Abū Nu'aim, "Delā'il Al-Nubūwwah" §§ 22, 23. A Jewess named Zainab attempted to poison the Prophet at Khaibar by dressing a kid, and having steeped it in deadly poison placed it before the Prophet, who ate but a mouthful when the deed was discovered. Zainab was immediately put to death (Hughes' *Dictionary of Islam*).

If one comes to you demanding the time and the story of the Kings,
Tell him that the Sun of al-Ghūrī has set, and the Sun of Ibn 'Othmān has risen.
This was the decree of the God of Heaven, and the world goes round for ever.

AN ACCOUNT OF THE REIGN OF ASHRAF ABU AL-NAṢR ṬŪMĀN BAI

This Sulṭān was the 47th of the Turkish Kings and their sons in Egypt, and the 21st of the Circassian Kings and their sons. He was originally one of the slaves of Ashraf Ḳāit Bai, having been purchased by the Sulṭān Ḳānṣūh al-Ghūrī, whose protection he sought on grounds of relationship. After purchasing him the Sulṭān presented him to Ḳāit Bai, for which reason he was called Tūmān Bai " Min "[1] Ḳānṣūh. He became one of his Kitabi Memlooks,[2] and retained this position until the accession of Malik Nāṣir Muḥammed Ibn Ḳāit Bai, who gave him horses, uniform, and slave boys, and he became one of the persons promoted by al-Nāṣir. For some time he was a page in waiting, then one of the personal suite, remaining in this position until the accession of his kinsman Ḳānṣūh al-Ghūrī. This latter conferred on him the rank of a Decurion, which he retained until the year A.H. 910; then when the Sulṭān's son died the Sulṭān gave him the Emirate of the Ṭablkhānāh, and made him keeper of the cellars in the place of his deceased son.

In this post he remained until the year A.H. 913, but when the Amīr Azdamar Ibn 'Alī Bai, Chie Dfawādār, died, in the month Jumādā al-Ūlā, whilst travelling in Jebel Nābulus, the Sulṭān gave him a robe of honour, and made him Chief Dawādār instead of the deceased Amīr. He kept this office

[1] For use of "Min" see Sobernheim's article on Jānbalāt in *Encyclopædia of Islam*.

[2] From ii, 92, it appears that these were Memlooks who were on a register.

until the Sulṭān left on his expedition against Ibn 'Othmān, when he was made Viceroy during the Sulṭān's absence [69]. He conducted the government during this time extremely well; the people were contented and the troops left behind in Egypt obeyed him. He combined the offices of Chief Dawādār, Lord High Chamberlain, Chief Inspector, and Viceroy. He used to ride out towards the Maṭariyyeh every Monday and Thursday, passing through Cairo after entering it by the Bāb al-Naṣr. He was preceded by a strong force of soldiers and chief Amīrs, by runners and slaves who fired naptha from instruments, and there was great commotion in Cairo as he passed through. He also opened the dam in the Sulṭān's absence, which occasion was observed as a public holiday.

[Here follows the story already told on p. 57 of the chöice of Ṭūmān Bai to be Sulṭān and his refusal, and of the Amīrs referring the matter to Sheikh Abū Su'ūd.]

Ṭūmān Bai pleaded a variety of excuses—that there was no money in the Treasury, so he could not spend anything on the Army; that Ibn 'Othmān was master of Syria and was advancing on Egypt, while the Amīrs would not consent to go upon a second expedition. He also said that if he became Sulṭān they would betray and depose him, and imprison him in the frontier town at Alexandria, and only retain him on the throne for a short time. Then followed the administering of an oath of fidelity to the Amīrs, and the acceptance of the sovereignty by Ṭūmān Bai. On Friday, the 14th of Ramaḍān of this year, after saying the early morning prayers, the Dawādār, accompanied by the chief Amīrs, and preceded by men carrying lamps and torches, rode up to the Bāb al-Silsilah and took up a position there. He had started from his house in the Bābāshaḳ road by the Ṣalībah Gate, wearing a light turban and a white cape—the Amīrs accompanying him being similarly dressed—and being greeted as he passed by voices praying for blessings on him, and by cheers from the women at their windows. On arrival at the Bāb al-Silsilah he sent for the Amīr of the Faithful

Ya'ḳūb, father of the Amīr of the Faithful al-Mutewekkil 'alā Allāh. The Amīr attended at the summons, accompanied by Seyyid Hārūn, son of the Khalīfah Muḥammed al-Mutewekkil 'alā Allāh, and their cousins the children of Khalīl.

Others attended with a number of Deputy Judges from Cairo. [Names omitted.]

* * * * *

When all were assembled, including the chief Amīrs and others of high or low rank, and the troops, Amīr of the Faithful Ya'ḳūb produced an authority from his son Muḥammed al-Mutewekkil to represent him, with full powers [70] in all matters concerning either himself or the Khalifate. He had sent confirmation of this by the hand of Ḳāḍī Shems al-Dīn Ibn Waḥīsh. This was accepted as correct. It had been rumoured that the Khalifate would be conferred on one of the sons of Seyyid Khalīl, since the Khalīfah al-Mutewekkil 'alā Allāh was a prisoner in the hands of Ibn 'Othmān, and his father Ya'ḳūb had abdicated the Khalifate, but when this document was produced bearing the authority of his son the people were satisfied.

Others also, being prisoners in the hands of Ibn 'Othmān, were not present at the ceremony of swearing allegiance. [Names omitted.]

* * * * *

None of the distinguished Shāfi'ī deputies were present at this ceremony except Sherefī Yaḥyā Ibn Burdīnī.

The oath was administered to the Sulṭān by the Khalīfah Amīr al-Mu'minīn Ya'ḳūb, and witnessed by Sherefī Yaḥyā Ibn Burdīnī, and a number of deputy judges representing Muḥammed al-Mutewekkil, the chief Ḥanefī Judge Muḥammed Ibn Shaḥna also attended at the close of the ceremony.

As soon as the oath had been taken the royal insignia were brought to the Sulṭān, that is to say, the black cloak, the black turban, and the Bedawī sword. The rites of investiture were completely performed; he assumed the title of al-Malik al-Ashraf like his kinsman al-Ghūrī. Then his special charger was brought up without either horse-cloth or gilt saddle, nor could they find for him in the armouries either parasol or bird, or gold drapery.

The Sulṭān rode from the Ḥarrāḳah steps at the Silsilah Gate, preceded by the Khalīfah, and went into the Great Palace by the private gate, and there took his seat on the imperial throne. Then the Amīrs kissed the ground before him, and the glad tidings were sounded from the citadel. His name was proclaimed in Cairo, voices were raised in prayer for him, and there was no one who was not glad at his accession. Being gentle, he was beloved by the people, and being free from pride he desired harm to no man. After the oath-taking the Sulṭān conferred a robe of honour on the Amīr al-Mu'minīn, and went down to his palace in the midst of a grand procession.

Thus ended the reign of al-Ghūrī. Praise be to Him whose kingdom never wanes; and to quote the words of Muḥammed Ibn Ḳānṣūh: "Al-Ghūrī has gone to his Lord in obedience to the decree of Allāh, to whom kingdoms belong, and to the sovereignty of which he appoints of his servants whom he wills."

At prayer-time on that Friday the Sulṭān (Ṭūmān Bai) went out to prayers, and his name was mentioned in the sermon by Sherefī Yaḥyā Ibn Burdīnī, and likewise on succeeding Fridays. Moreover, the preachers made reference to the Sulṭān in their sermons on that day from the pulpits in the mosques in Cairo; for the previous fifty days no Sulṭān's name had been thus mentioned, nor prayers offered for him, but only for the Khalīfah.

On this day the Sulṭān arrested Ḳānṣūh al-Ashrafī, Governor of the Citadel of Aleppo, who had surrendered without resistance to Ibn 'Othmān. So when this Ḳānṣūh attended under escort the Sulṭān expressed his displeasure, and ordered his confinement in the Citadel Tower, until his wishes concerning him should be made known.

On Saturday, the 15th of Ramaḍān, there arrived a number

of Amīrs, who had remained behind at Damascus after the troops had left. Amongst these were (1) Amīr Jān Birdī al-Ghazālī, Governor of Ḥamāh; he had aspired to the governorship of Damascus; (2) Amīr Sūdūn Dawādār, [71] Chief of the Corps of Guards; (3) Amīr Ḳanṣūh Kurt, one of the chief Amīrs, who arrived sick. On their arrival they found that the Dawādār [Ṭūmān Bai] had succeeded to the throne. This gave offence to Amīr Sūdūn, the Dawādār, who, whilst he was absent in Syria, had been counting on becoming Sulṭān himself. His wish, however, was not realized.

On their arrival they went up to the citadel, made their obeisance to the Sulṭān, and then went to their homes.

Then came news from the Amīr of the Arabs of Ḥamāh, Amīr Nāṣir al-Dīn Ibn al-Ḥanash, that Ibn ʻOthmān had sent a detachment under Ibn Suwār, who had declared his allegiance to him. At Ḳābūn, near Damascus, they were met by Ibn Ḥanash, and a bloody battle ensued, in which a number of Ibn ʻOthmān's men were killed. The rivers of Damascus were let loose against them, their horses stuck fast in the mud, and a great number of them perished in this way, as told by the reports received. Then I wrote :—

> Tell Ibn ʻOthmān, if you meet him, to take advice,
> Not to be rash and to beware,
> Lest he withstand a Syrian without due forethought,
> And run against the sting of Ibn Ḥanash.

Along with the Amīrs many of the notables of Damascus came with their families, for after the defeat of the army and the death of Sī Bai, the Governor, confusion reigned there. Some of the people of the city attacked the others, plundering the brokers' quarter, killing a number of persons, and taking their property. The Frank merchants were similarly treated, and terrible riots prevailed. The judges and leading native merchants of Damascus had their houses pillaged, and this and the troubles caused by Ibn ʻOthmān, and the general ruin of affairs in Egypt and Syria led to the quitting of the city by the majority of them.

When the Sulṭān learnt of the success of Nāṣir al-Dīn Ibn Ḥanash against the troops of Ibn 'Othmān, he appointed him Governor of Ḥomṣ. It was said that imperial instructions were sent to him to the effect that if he could defeat Ibn 'Othmān's army the Sulṭān would make him Atābek of Damascus; and that Ibn al-Ḥanash replied that if the Sulṭān would assist him with troops, he would collect a force of Arabs and personally guarantee the defeat of Ibn 'Othmān's army. One of al-Ḥanash's ancestors was formerly Governor of Ḥomṣ.

On the same day a person named Īnāl, the squint-eyed, arrived. He had been appointed Deputy of Ṣafad by Jān Birdī al-Ghazālī. On sending his Dawādār and executive officials to Ṣafad they were attacked by the inhabitants, and not allowed to enter the town, and some, it appears, were killed. So he went to Egypt to be invested, meaning to return and take revenge on the people of Ṣafad.

On Monday, the 17th, the Sulṭān paid the troops in his private grounds. On the same day there arose a dispute among the Amīrs as to their various offices; there was also a quarrel between Amīr 'Allān, the Sub-Dawādār and Jān Birdī al-Ghazālī, in which both parties overstepped the bounds of moderation. Then the Sulṭān gave orders for the inspection of the troops who had not taken part in the expedition, but remained behind in Egypt. He also proclaimed that any one who had taken possession of arms or clothing belonging to the troops was to restore them at once, under penalty, if denounced, of immediate death by
[72] hanging. Information had reached him that a number of servants and slaves on the expedition had stolen many things in the shape of money, arms, uniforms, etc.

Amongst matters of less consequence it may be mentioned that the Sulṭān, on his accession, ordered the stone seat to be pulled down which al-Ghūrī had put up in his private grounds, in place of the dais[1] which Ashraf Ḳāit Bai used to sit on ; so the stone seat was replaced by the dais once more, and the Sulṭān used it. It had been broken, but he had it repaired, and made a yellow cloth covering for it. He used it as a judgment seat for hearing trials, like Ashraf Ḳāit Bai, and I said :—

The Dais of Justice has come back,
The "Masṭabah" of Injustice has been pulled down ;
Ṭūmān Bai has become amongst the people
As one who causes the wolf to live with the sheep in peace.
Oh ! what a King he is ! his justice has become notorious
Amongst Arabs, and people of other countries.

On Tuesday, the 18th, the Sulṭān sat on the dais and reviewed the troops in his private grounds, and enrolled about two thousand Memlooks, and gave appointments to some six chief Amīrs who were in Cairo. He gave the command of the troops to Amīr Jān Birdī al-Ghazālī, who had aspired to be Governor of Damascus. On the same day the Sulṭān arrested the Mihtār Muḥammed Fujūlī and his brother 'Alī, Superintendent of the Wardrobe in the service of the Sulṭān al-Ghūrī. He also arrested Jemāl al-Dīn al-Alwāḥī, Guardian at Dahīshah. This was the Sulṭān Ṭūmān Bai's first judgment, given for the following reason. When he came to the throne he inspected the treasuries and found them empty, with neither a dīnār nor a dirhem in them. The Sulṭān al-Ghūrī had, on the death of Amīr Khāir Bey, appointed these two, Muḥammed the Superintendent and Jemāl al-Dīn the Guardian, as financial advisers, and they did as they pleased with the money. They became insolent and interfered in affairs which were out of their province, never thinking that the Sulṭān al-Ghūrī would die when he did ; and it was this belief of theirs that was one of the chief causes of their ruin. Some one rightly said : "These are things to make fools laugh, and the wise to weep at their consequences."

[1] Platform, high wooden sofa.

On Thursday, the 20th, the Sulṭān held a grand full dress court, he himself being seated on the dais in his private grounds, and conferred robes of honour on about twenty Amīrs [names omitted].

* * * * *

[73] On Tuesday, the 25th, the Sulṭān conferred a robe of honour on the Sheikh of the Arabs, Amīr Aḥmed Ibn Baḳar, and confirmed him in his appointment. The tribe of the Amīr had committed excesses during this year, such as do not occur at the hands of the Franks, murdering people and plundering property. Notable outrages were committed by Ibn al-Judhāmī on the troops returning after their defeat, and by the tribe of ‘Abd al-Dā’im in the east of the country, in the shape of plunder and murder, and no one troubled himself about it. However, a robe of honour was conferred on the Sheikh, and no more was heard of these doings.

On Thursday, the 27th, the Sulṭān gave robes of honour to several Amīrs [names omitted].

* * * * *

[74] On Saturday, the 29th, the Inspector of the Sulṭān's private domain came up with the festival robes and displayed them to the Sulṭān, spread out over the heads of the porters.

On Sunday, the last day of the month, Nāṣirī Muḥammed Ibn Bal Bai al-Mu'eyyed from Damascus arrived with the news that Selīm Shāh Ibn ‘Othmān had taken possession of the city and citadel and had killed ‘Alī Bai al-Ashrafī, Governor of the citadel, and thirty-six Amīrs of Damascus, besides some of the Sulṭān's subjects living there. This Ibn Bal Bai arrived dressed as an Arab, with a native cloak and head-dress.

When it became known in Cairo that Ibn ‘Othmān was in possession of Damascus the people were terror-stricken, and said that it would be Egypt's turn next. They were firmly convinced that it would come to this, and some determined to fly to Upper Egypt. Both the Sulṭān and the Amīrs and all the people were much disturbed at this news, especially as it was the eve of the "Festival of Fiṭr", and the sorrows of the people were still fresh, owing to the death of the Sulṭān, the defeat of the army, and the mourning for the men who had fallen. And I said :—

O Ibn 'Othmān, desist from taking Egypt,
The land which is dignified with the best of Imāms;
Our chief Imām is al-Shāfi'ī, a Polestar and a saint,
The son of Idrīs, a pillar of Islām.
She is called the Quiver, and whoever attacks her—
God will break his back with a sword.

On Monday, the first day of Shawwāl, the Sulṭān offered up the festival prayer, and conferred robes of honour on the Amīrs and the usual persons. The Sharafī Yahyā Ibn al-Burdīnī mentioned the Sulṭān's name in the Khutba, and a grand festival procession took place. On Friday, the 5th, corresponding to the 4th of the Coptic month "Hātūr", the Sulṭān exchanged his linen clothes for woollen; he did this too hastily.

On this day Amīr Jānem al-Ibrāhīmī, one of the Amīrs of the Ṭablkhānāh, died.

On Saturday, the 6th, two persons named 'Alī Sha'bānī, the deputy of the Muḥtesib, and Ibn Khabīz, the corn-broker, came to the Sulṭān and pointed out to him that if he were to impose a fixed rate on the market dues and on the crops it would be no hardship to the Faithful. But the Sulṭān would not hear them, and flogged them both. He publicly exposed Sha'bānī in Cairo, causing him to walk bareheaded, and to be beaten as he went; whilst a crier proclaimed this to be the punishment for trying to re-establish unjust measures [75] under a just government, after they had been repealed. The Sulṭān then ordered Sha'bānī to be dismissed from the office of adviser about the control of the market, and it was reported that he died from the blows he had received.

On Monday, the 8th, the Dawādār deputy of Gaza, known as 'Alī Bey, the hunchback, arrived with the news that Ibn 'Othmān had suffered a set-back since his entry into Damascus. Disease was rife amongst his troops, deaths occurring daily.

He also said that there was a scarcity of grain and fodder, that the Arabs were endeavouring to stop the supply of barley, wheat, and straw, and that when any of the soldiers went out into the villages they were killed by the Arabs. Ibn 'Othmān had penetrated so far that he could not withdraw; his cavalry horses were roaming about eating the leaves of trees, and were much emaciated. On the same day Khudā Birdī, Governor of Alexandria, also arrived; he had gone there to carry out what had been settled; and Amīr Khāir Bey, the architect, also arrived. He had been to the fortress of Rashīd to see about the repair of the wall and the towers.

On the same day the Sulṭān conferred a robe of honour on a Turk named Māl Bai al-Musharref, and appointed him to be personal steward instead of Ḳānṣūh al-Ashrafī, killed in the engagement with Ibn 'Othmān.

On Tuesday, the 9th, a quarrel occurred between al-Zeinī Berekāt Ibn Mūsā and Sheikh Abū al-Su'ūd, which arose thus. A certain tanner and dealer in skins named Damrāwī agreed about the sale of some skins; Ibn Mūsā acted wrongfully towards him, and a quarrel was started between them. Ibn Mūsā determined to arrest him. Then Damrāwī went to Sheikh Abū al-Su'ūd and implored his protection. The latter sent an abusive letter to Ibn Mūsā on the subject, which he took no notice of, but kept him waiting about the matter.

Then the Sheikh summoned Ibn Mūsā, and on his appearing before him at Kaum al-Jāriḥ the Sheikh reproved him sharply, saying: "You dog, how you do oppress the Faithful!" This infuriated Ibn Mūsā, who left his presence in anger. So the Sheikh ordered his head to be uncovered, and that he be beaten with shoes on the head and body till he nearly died. Then after securing him he sent for Amīr 'Allān, the Chief Dawādār, and said to him, "Put him in irons and go and consult the Sulṭān about him, and inform him that the man is injuring the Faithful." The Sulṭān on hearing the case sent to Sheikh Abu Su'ūd, telling him to act as he thought fit in the matter. The latter ordered Ibn Mūsā to be publicly exposed in Cairo and then hung at the Zawīlah Gate. Ibn Mūsā was then brought out from the Sheikh's quarters at Kaum al-Jāriḥ, walking bareheaded and in irons. It was publicly proclaimed that this was the punishment of a man who oppressed the Faithful. He was thus escorted to the confines of Old Cairo, till at last they reached Amīr 'Allān, the Dawādār's, house at Nāṣiriyyeh. He desired to sign his death-warrant by hanging or drowning, but the people pointed out to the Sheikh that he owed the Sulṭān money, and that if he were hung the Sulṭān would forfeit it. So the Sheikh repealed the death-sentence, and Ibn Mūsā remained in irons at Amīr 'Allān's residence. Thus the affair between Ibn Mūsā and Sheikh Abū al-Su'ūd was attended with grave consequences, which nearly culminated in the execution of the former.

* * * * *

[76] After all this trouble of Ibn Mūsā's an enemy of his named Shihāb al-Dīn Ibn al-Ṣā'igh appeared upon the scene. He had taken steps against Ibn Mūsā during al-Ghūrī's reign; and when this affair occurred he again brought up a charge. So he said, "I can bear witness to a debt of Ibn Mūsā's to the Sulṭān to the extent of 100,000 dīnars." Then Ibn al-Ṣā'igh went to Ibn Mūsā's house, accompanied by eunuchs and kavasses and a great many others, and attacked and arrested Ibn Mūsā's women, plundering their house property and laying hands on his slaves, servants, and retainers.

When the Sulṭān heard this he gave up persecuting Ibn Mūsā, who then said that he could bear witness to a debt of 200,000 dīnārs against Ibn al-Ṣā'igh, so the Sulṭān told Amīr 'Allān to send for Ibn al-Ṣā'igh and have him put in irons until he should have settled his accounts. As to Sheikh Abū al-Su'ūd, a storm of indignation arose against him, on account of his treatment of Ibn Mūsā, and the poor people and others found fault with him, saying, "What business has the Sheikh to interfere in the Sulṭān's affairs."

On Sunday, the 14th, the Princess, who was the daughter

of Amīr Aḳ Birdī, the Dawādār, and wife of the Sulṭān, went up to the citadel; her mother was the daughter of Khāṣṣ Bey and sister of Ashraf Ḳāit Bai's wife. She went up at the time of morning prayers, with lanterns and torches, accompanied by a great number of princesses and ladies, and the wives of Amīrs and executive officers. They formed a procession until they reached the citadel, where she entered the Hall of Columns. The chief eunuch of the bedchamber staff held over her head the Umbrella and Bird[1] until she took her seat on the throne. This day was observed in her honour, as one of special celebrations at the citadel.

On Sunday, the Amīr 'Allān, the Dawādār, paraded Ibn Mūsā and Ibn Ṣā'igh. A sum of 20,000 dīnārs had been assessed against Ibn Mūsā, of which amount half was to be applied to salaries, but he produced none of it. So the Amīr threw him down and beat him about twenty times, after which he promised to produce the amount. Then the Amīr summoned Aḥmed Ibn al-Ṣā'igh and beat him over four hundred times, from which he nearly died; his death, in fact, was reported amongst the people.

On Thursday, the 18th, the Maḥmal (the Holy Carpet) was not dispatched from Cairo; no one, in fact, made the pilgrimage owing to the disturbance caused by the rebellion of Ibn 'Othmān. It was reported that he was going to send a number of his soldiers to Mecca, with coverings for the [77] Ka'bah, but this was not confirmed. Then the Sulṭān sent the eunuch Murhef by sea with the coverings for the Ka'bah, and the purses for the people of Mecca and Medina; so he proceeded to Sinai, and down to the sea from there.

On Friday, the 19th, it was reported that Sheikh Abū al-Su'ūd had sent and released Ibn Mūsā from irons, and showed that he had pardoned him, and he began to interfere in political matters, and the people disapproved of this. On

[1] Al Ḳubbah wa Al Ṭair, a term "applied by historians to an umbrella surmounted by the figure of a bird which was borne over the head of a Sultan in certain pompous processions." (Lane's *Modern Egyptians*.)

Saturday, the 20th, Zeynī Berekāt Ibn Mūsā went to the Sulṭān requesting him to restore him to his office; but the Sulṭān paid no heed so he left him without effecting his purpose, and remained under observation until he should have completely satisfied the claims against him. He returned home greatly humiliated, after his quarters in the Milk Market had been illuminated in his honour and his adherents had perfumed themselves with saffron. Consequently they were much discouraged.

On Sunday, the 21st, the Sulṭān conferred a robe of honour on Sheref al-Dīn Ibn 'Ivaḍ, and appointed him to be controller of the Treasury instead of Ibn Mūsā dismissed from this office.

On Monday, the 22nd, the Sulṭān sent instructions to the troops that on Tuesday the first instalment of pay would be issued. On the same day news came from India [1] that the ships which the Sulṭān al-Ghūrī had dispatched had gone down with all guns and arms and other things on board. A quarrel had arisen between the commander, Salmān al-Othmānī, and the local governor, al-Amīr Ḥusein of Jeddah, and that each of them had gone to a different part of India.

On the same day the Sulṭān conferred a robe of honour on a Turk, Ḳajmās, formerly Steward in Benhā al-'Asel, and appointed him to the Inspectorate of the Sharkiyyeh Province, after cancelling the previous appointment. The Sulṭān also issued pay to the troops detailed for active service, giving to each Memlook fifty dīnārs. This they returned to him, and jabbered and went out of the gate of the grounds in a rage, intending to raise a revolt. But some of the Amīrs advised the Sulṭān to appease them by paying them a hundred dīnārs each, as usual. So the angry soldiers were recalled, and on their return the Sulṭān paid each Memlook a hundred dīnārs, and three months' pay, amounting to one hundred

[1] "Hind," according to Moslem geographers, was Southern India, including the Indian Archipelago, with a part of Southern China, and thence across the Indian Ocean to the east coast of Africa.

and twenty dīnārs. On that day he paid the men of four barracks. It was reported that these troops were to march out to Gaza with the Amīrs, and to occupy the town until the departure of the great expedition in the spring. At this time the Sulṭān sent to arrest a number of Greeks of Khān al-Khalīlī, said to be corresponding with Ibn 'Othmān about Egyptian affairs, and to have spies with them from him. On arrest he put them in irons. The Sulṭān was reported to have summoned the little boy, called Ḳāsim Ibn Aḥmed Bey Ibn 'Othmān, who had accompanied al-Ghūrī on the expedition. After the defeat of the army he had returned with the Amīrs to Egypt, and having heard of a plot against him the Sulṭān had fears for his life, so he brought him up to the citadel and gave him quarters by the reservoir, allowing him and his suite a competence.

At this time Sherefī Yaḥyā Ibn al-Atābek Ezbek Ibn Ṭaṭakh arrived in Cairo. He had been living at Ḥamāh, [78] but fled thence when the place was captured by Ibn 'Othmān, and came to Egypt by sea from Tripoli.

The Sulṭān conferred a robe of honour on Amīr Ṭaḳt Bai, Chief Chamberlain, and appointed him as adviser in the Inspectorate of Buḥairah instead of Yūsuf al-Bedrī, in addition to the duties of his office.

On Friday, the 26th, Ḳāḍi 'Abd al-Kerīm Ibn al-Jī'ān, brother of Shihābī Aḥmed Ibn al-Jī'ān, arrived in Cairo. He had been a prisoner with Ibn 'Othmān in Syria, but escaped into Egypt disguised as a camel-driver, wearing an Arab cloak and a skull-cap. He was accompanied by Aḥmed al-Dimyāṭī, a merchant in al-Warrākīn. He informed the Sūlṭān that Ibn 'Othmān's power had waned, that his troops were at variance with him, that his communications had been cut by Nāṣir al-Dīn Ibn al-Ḥanash, and that the Arabs were killing isolated soldiers in the villages. He also told that Ibn 'Othmān had taken possession of the town of Damascus and its citadel, and the citadel of Tripoli and Ṣafad and their provinces, and was master of the country from

Damascus to the Euphrates. A number of his Amīrs had been made governors in the towns he had captured, as in Aleppo, Ḥamāh, Ḥomṣ, and other towns. It was said that Ibn al-Ḥanash had sent an official communication to the Sulṭān to urge him to dispatch an expedition quickly, before Ibn 'Othmān had time to advance on Gaza. Then the Sulṭān conferred a robe of honour on Ḳāḍī 'Abd al-Kerīm, and went down to his house.

On Monday, the 29th, the Sulṭān gave a robe of honour to the son of the successor of Seyyid Aḥmed al-Bedawī, who had been killed by Ibn 'Othmān in Aleppo, and appointed him in his father's stead. The newly appointed successor left the citadel with a great procession with banners held above him, and preceded by all the Aḥmadiyyeh dervishes.

After the conferring of the appointments they went down to the citadel, wearing their badges of honour, and were received with loud acclamations by the people of Cairo, who lined the streets to view the procession. These judges assumed their offices at a time when Cairo was in extreme consternation on account of Ibn 'Othmān.

On the same day the Sulṭān gave the final instalment of pay to the troops detailed for the expedition, and the latter began to make their preparations for departure to Gaza. It was said that the Sulṭān paid about 2,000 of these Memlooks.

On Friday Malik al-'Umarā Jān Birdī al-Ghazālī, Governor of Damascus, went up to the citadel and joined the Sulṭān in the Friday prayers. Then the Sulṭān conferred on him a robe of honour and gave him the rank of Pasha in command of the troops detailed for the expedition. On leaving the citadel the Pasha went to his tent at Raidānniyyeh, [79] leaving the city without a regular procession, being preceded merely by some led horses, drummers, and torch-bearers and going before the Amīrs and troops.

On Saturday, the 5th, the Sulṭān ordered the expeditionary troops to leave the city that day, in order to join the Pasha, saying that whoever failed to start would be dealt with accordingly. However, a number of Memlooks appeared before him refusing to start until he paid them six Ashrafis, the price of a camel, and issued forage to them and meat ration money. This caused some excitement, and the Sulṭān left the assembly objecting to the claim. The troops were dissatisfied, affairs were unsettled, and Ibn 'Othmān was advancing on Gaza; the Governor was asking for the dispatch of troops before Ibn 'Othmān should capture the town of Gaza, and thus cause the Sulṭān the trouble of recapturing the country.

On Sunday, the 6th, one of the Amīrs, commanders of a thousand, of the expeditionary force left the city. He was daily followed into camp by others, the Pasha in command, Jān Birdī, remaining at Raidāniyyeh until the whole force should be complete.

On Monday, the 7th, the Sultan paid three months rations to the expeditionary troops; each Memlook also received about four and a half Ashrafis apiece as an extra gratuity.

On the same day arrived two of the Royal Memlooks, who had been in some of the villages with the Arabs, returning to Egypt disguised as servants. They brought the same stories of Ibn 'Othmān's difficulties that had been told before [see p. 83], and some said that Khāir Bey had been killed. This had no foundation in fact.

On Wednesday, the 9th, the Dawādār of Khāir Bey, the Governor of Aleppo, arrived; he had made his escape from Ibn 'Othmān. He brought the news that Ibn 'Othmān had dispatched a force of about five thousand cavalry under Ibn Suwār, who was on the point of taking Gaza; in fact, according to some accounts he had actually taken it, and the Governor of Gaza was reported to have fled.

This intelligence caused great consternation; the Sulṭān was deeply distressed; he gave orders for the force to march immediately, and that any absentees should receive the punishment deserved. On Thursday the troops marched off in hot haste. The Sulṭān also started, accompanied by all the Amīrs, and people said that it was the Sulṭān himself who would encounter Ibn 'Othmān. The Sulṭān took with him the Governor of Aleppo, the great Amīr, in irons, and a number of the bodyguard of Gaza, also in irons. The Governor of Gaza had reported against them that they had corresponded with Ibn 'Othmān, suggesting to him that he should come and take possession of Gaza unopposed. They, however, denied this before the Sulṭān, and said that Dolāt Bey, the Governor, had a grudge against the Gaza guards, and had invented this false story against them.

The Sulṭān then gave them credit for speaking the truth, and sent Jān Birdī, Governor of Damascus, to acquit them of the idle charge made against them. The Sulṭān released those that were with him, and sent them to the Inspector-General of the army to have their cases inquired into.

[80] On Friday, the 11th, further rumours were current to the effect that Ibn 'Othmān had sent troops to Gaza, under the command of his Amīrs, one of whom was Iskender Pasha and another Dā'ūd Pasha. It was also reported that they had captured Gaza, and burnt some of the houses that the Governor had fled, that Ibn 'Othmān's troops were advancing on Egypt, and that affairs were in a bad way.

When the Sulṭān felt convinced of the truth of this news it was reported that he would himself go out to meet Ibn 'Othmān. He gave orders that the roughs, the mischievous boys, the maghribis, and whosoever was in hiding on account of a murder or was blood-guilty would receive a pardon on presenting himself. He would inspect them on the Maidān, and give them pay and an animal to ride, and they would be attached to the corps of armourers during the Sulṭān's advance. This proclamation gave offence to the people, who did not like his pardoning murderers; it would have been better to have said nothing about this.

Complete confusion prevailed on that day throughout Cairo; the expeditionary soldiers left in a great hurry. Amīr

Khudā Birdī al-Ashrafī, one of the chief Amīrs, formerly Governor of Alexandria, also left. He had no regular state-procession, but was preceded by led chargers, and escorted by a large body of his Memlook troops; some said three hundred Memlooks. All the people invoked blessings on his head, and prayed for victory for the troops, being terror-stricken on account of Ibn 'Othmān.

On Saturday, the 12th, the Sulṭān sitting on the dais in his grounds received the Amīrs and urged them to leave the city that day. Then Amīr Ṭaḳṭ Bai, the Chief Chamberlain, said that he had decided to go to Buḥairah, as he had been appointed Inspector there. To this the Amīrs replied that it was much more important for him to go out to fight Ibn 'Othmān than to go to Buḥairah, and they further told him that he did not go out with the Sulṭān al-Ghūrī when he went on his expedition, and that he had not been plundered of baggage and uniform. To this the Amīr made excuse that he was not well. A great quarrel ensued between them in the presence of the Sulṭān, and finally the imported Memlooks planned to go and pillage and burn his house. Some of the Memlooks are said to have struck him, and he suffered great indignities at their hands. Ultimately he agreed to accompany the Amīrs on the expedition, and the Sulṭān prevented the Memlooks from plundering his house.

On that day the Sulṭān ordered the whole of the troops to parade for inspection; also the Amīr, who had been made Governor of Ḥamāh instead of Jān Birdi al-Ghazālī, left the city with a military escort.

That day Amīr Erzamak Nāshif, one of the chief Amīrs, also left the city. He formed a regular military procession, and was preceded by led horses and two drums, and had a banner held above his head. The Amīrs gradually left the city to join in the fighting against Ibn 'Othmān.

On Sunday, the 13th, the Sulṭān reviewed the expeditionary troops in the Maidān. He went through the enrolment list a second time, and only exempted a small number. He also inspected four barracks and registered most of the Memlooks in them for the expedition.

The same day the Sulṭān inspected a wooden vehicle drawn [81] by oxen, and carrying musketeers; there were about thirty or more of these vehicles. He also inspected camels carrying an arrangement for musketeers to shoot from, on their backs, also wooden shields as a protection against arrows. So the troops that day felt in good heart for the fight. The Sulṭān declared that he was going in person to take part in the battle against Ibn ʻOthmān, and he urged the rest of the Amīrs to leave with all haste for the fray. But he gave them no money, saying that they must go out and fight for themselves, their children, and their wives. "There is nothing left," he said, "in the Treasury; I am one of yourselves; if you go out, I go with you; and if you sit still, I sit still with you; I have no money to give you."

On Monday, the 14th, it was reported that the Sulṭān had become displeased with Zeinī Berekāt Ibn Mūsā, and had restored him to internment, after he had seemed likely to be restored to his office. The Sulṭān had charged Ibn Mūsā with the payment of a certain sum, of which he produced only a small amount, pleading inability to pay more. When the soldiers had to be paid previous to their hasty departure, the Sulṭān put pressure on those who had debts owing, of whom were Ibn Mūsā, and Muḥammed, the Superintendent, and Jemāl al-Dīn, Guardian of Dahīshah, and others, from whom arrears of money were due to help towards the payment of the soldiers.

On the same day Amīr Ḳānṣūh al-Fājir, one of the chief Amīrs, left the city to proceed on the expedition; also Amīr Ṭaḳṭ Bai, Chief Chamberlain. The latter had a procession, two drums and fifes, and some led horses going before him, like Erzamak al-Nāshif.

On Tuesday, the 15th, the Sulṭān inspected the remainder of the troops in the Maidān, and ordered the Amīrs with all the troops who were still left to start forthwith under penalties for disobedience. So the expeditionary army left in mid-winter, and suffered great hardships in consequence. On this day Tānī Bey Nejmī, one of the chief Amīrs, left, having the recognized war procession.

On Thursday, the 17th, Amīr Elmās, Vālī of Cairo, started. Also on this day a foreigner, a sausage-maker, was arrested; he was found to have taken a fat black dog, and to have killed it, and made it into sausages. On his arrest he was taken before Amīr Māmāī, the Inspector of Markets, who caused him to be beaten with rods, and publicly exposed in Cairo, with the dog hung round his neck. After taking him round the town, he was imprisoned at Makshara. The Franks had been constantly committing atrocious acts of this nature.

On Monday, 21st, this occurrence took place: certain of the royal Memlooks on their way out towards Maṭariyyeh saw a party coming towards them from the direction of Birkah al-Ḥāj. These people when questioned said that they were emissaries from the Sulṭān Selīm Shāh Ibn 'Othmān; they were about fifteen in number. The chief emissary was an old, white-bearded man, dressed in velvet. In their company was also a man from Egypt, 'Abd al-Barr Ibn Maḥāsin, who had been Treasury Secretary to Atābek Sūdūn al-Ajemī. When the latter was killed [82], and Ibn 'Othmān took Aleppo and Damascus, the secretary was won over by the influence of Yūnus al-Ādilī and al-Samarḳandī. When Ibn 'Othmān sent these emissaries they dared not come by Gaza, as the Governor of Damascus, Jān Birdī al-Ghazālī, was in the vicinity besieging a force of Ibn 'Othmān's which was in Gaza. So they bribed some Arabs with a substantial sum to take them by the Sultān's road. This brought them by the desert to Ajrūd, and before people were aware of their arrival they were in the centre of the town. The Memlooks, on meeting them, arrested the chief emissary and his party, including Maḥāsin and the three Arabs with them. Meanwhile, they were approached by three Greeks from Khān al-Khalīlī, who saluted them and kissed their hands. The Memlooks promptly arrested them, and asked how they knew that the emissaries were coming on this day, and said that they were spies of Ibn 'Othmān's. After beating them they brought them to the house of Amīr 'Allān, the great Dawādār. At the house they ordered the emissary to dismount and salute the Dawādār. This he refused to do, using violent language against them. He then drew his sword and threw himself on the Dawādār's people; seeing this the Dawādār ordered the Memlooks to compel him to dismount, who made him get off and took his sword from him. They then fell upon him and his Turkish companions, beat them, stripped them, and put them in irons, after subjecting them to outrageous insults.

When the Sulṭān heard of this he summoned Amīr Moghul Bai Dawādār Sikkīn, whom al-Ghūrī had sent to Ibn 'Othmān, and who had suffered abominable insults at the latter's hands. He was now ordered to go down, and to subject Ibn 'Othmān's emissary to the same treatment.

He took his comrades and went with them to Amīr 'Allān's house, with a view to subjecting them to insults or to killing them (?). But Amīr 'Allān would not suffer this.

Then they brought 'Abd al-Barr Ibn Maḥāsin to the Sulṭān, in whose presence he expatiated on the merits and the greatness of Ibn 'Othmān. He recounted how eight hundred Egyptians were beheaded by him in one day, on his entry into Aleppo, including the successor of the Seyyid Aḥmed al-Bedawī and other notables who had remained behind there. He further reported that the troops of Ibn 'Othmān amounted to over sixty thousand men; that the Khuṭbah was delivered in his name from Bagdad to Damascus, and that his coinage was current from Bagdad to Damascus. Also that on his entry into Syria he set about building a wall with towers from Ḳābūn to the extremity of Damascus, securing the town by gates in the walls; that he was animated by great enthusiasm, and boasted that he would not turn back till he had conquered Egypt and killed all the Circassian Memlooks there. He told how Ibn 'Othmān would remain in seclusion for a day at a time, while his soldiers killed the inhabitants and committed atrocities. He said that they did not fast during Ramaḍān, drank wine and būzah, and smoked ḥashīsh (?).

[83] Neither did Ibn 'Othmān say the Friday prayers except occasionally; these ugly stories had been circulated about him, independently of Ibn Mahāsin, by eye-witnesses of the doings of his troops in Aleppo and Damascus. After this long account of Ibn 'Othmān's actions, the Sulṭān said in a fit of anger, "You are a spy of Ibn 'Othmān's and have come here to obtain intelligence for him." He then ordered Ibn Maḥāsin's imprisonment in the citadel tower, where he remained some days, after which he was released at the intercession of Atābek Sūdūn, the Dawādār.

The hearts of the soldiers sank at this account. Then the Sulṭān ordered two of the Arabs to be hanged, who had guided the emissaries along their unknown route. It was also rumoured that a party of about forty of Ibn 'Othmān's men had come with them, and were hidden in Cairo.

On learning this the Sulṭān issued instructions to Khān al-Khalīlī that no one was to harbour any of Ibn 'Othmān's men, on pain of being hanged forthwith.

Then the Sulṭān sent for the letters brought by the emissaries, whom he had not given an interview. Amongst them were a number addressed to the Amīrs, executive officials, and Egyptian notables. It appeared after the Sulṭān's perusal of the letters that they were mostly expressed in Turkish, the purport of them being as follows: "From his Majesty to Amīr Ṭūmān Bai. It has been revealed to me that I shall become the possessor of the east and west, like Alexander the Great." Much of the letter consisted of threats and violent language, as for example: "You are a Memlook, who is bought and sold, you are not fit to govern. I am a king, descended through twenty generations of kings, and have taken possession of the country by agreement with the Khalīfah and the judges." After many similar expressions, the letter continued: "If you wish to escape violent treatment let an issue of coinage be struck in our name in Egypt, and let the Khuṭbah be delivered also in our name; and become our governor from Gaza to Egypt, while we will rule from Syria to the Euphrates. But if you do not obey us, then I will enter Egypt, and kill all the Circassians there, ripping open those with child and destroying the unborn." He made so great a display of grandeur and power that may be God will desert him on account of his excessive presumption.

When this letter was read to the Sulṭān he wept and was terrified. The imported Memlooks had agreed that if the emissary came up to the citadel they would fall upon him with their swords, so he did not appear there. The contents of Ibn 'Othmān's communication soon became known among the people, and led to great confusion. Everyone was on the watch for Ibn 'Othmān, saying: "As his emissaries came to us when we did not expect them, so he may fall upon us unexpectedly." People began to make strongholds for themselves in the neighbourhood of the city, where they might be hidden if Ibn 'Othmān entered Cairo. Others decided to take their families to Upper Egypt, should his approach be confirmed. A story was circulated that Khāir Bey, Governor of Aleppo, who had rebelled and submitted to Ibn 'Othmān, [84] had written to some of the chief Amīrs urging them to tender their submission to Ibn 'Othmān, extolling his virtues and just treatment of his subjects, and assuring them that if he came into Egypt they might all retain their posts and salaries. All this was mere trickery and deceit to facilitate Ibn 'Othmān's entry into Egypt.

Then the Sulṭān proclaimed that the next issue of pay would take place on Wednesday, the 23rd; he sat on the dais in his courtyard and the troops came up to receive it. Each Memlook had thirty dīnārs and three months' pay, amounting to twenty dīnārs; but they threw it down before him and said, "We will not start until we have received one hundred dīnārs apiece; moreover, we have neither horses, nor clothing, nor equipment, nor arms." They left the citadel in anger. The Sulṭān, extremely displeased, left the dais, and (? ? ?). He said "that he could not manage to pay one hundred dīnārs to each Memlook, for the state coffers were empty; that if they were not content they might elect whom they chose to be Sulṭān, and he would go to Mecca or elsewhere." So there were disturbances that day. It was reported that some Memlooks said to the Sulṭān himself, "If you are Sulṭān follow the custom of the former Sulṭāns; if you resign, may the curse of Allāh be upon you, and another will succeed you." The Sulṭān said to the troops, "You received thirty dīnārs from the Sulṭān al-Ghūrī, and then you did not fight, but forsook him and left him to his death." The troops went away in anger, and some said they quarrelled among themselves. On the same day the Sulṭān ordered all the Amīrs of rank to come up early the next day for a final parade; the meeting was then dissolved.

On Thursday, the 24th, the Sulṭān took his seat again on the dais, and all the Amīrs and troops assembled. Seyyid Muḥammed Ibn al-Sulṭān al-Ghūrī also attended, and the Sulṭān said: "Here is your Master's son, ask him if his father left any money in the Treasury; he will tell you, and if you like to make him Sulṭān, I will be the first to kiss the ground before him." To this the imported Memlooks replied, "We will march without pay, to avenge our Master." But the Ḳarāniṣah Memlooks said, "We will not march unless we receive one hundred and thirty dīnārs, like those who went on the former expedition." Then the meeting dispersed, many still murmuring, and there was much irresponsible talk that day. Some reported that the Amīrs said to the Sulṭān: "Do as al-Ashraf Ḳāit Bai and al-Ghūrī did; take money from the lands and pious foundations and endowments and fief-holders, and pay the army in that way, so as to keep the enemy out of Egypt." But the Sulṭān did not approve. "I will never introduce injustice," he said,

" during my government." This was gratefully acknowledged by the people, who blessed him for it. He would have been within his rights, and they would have excused him had he done it, as the object was to keep out their enemies, and he could have replenished his Treasury in this way. But God had disposed him to do good, and he will reap his reward for this hereafter.

[85] On the same day it was reported that the Sulṭān had sent to tell the adherents of Mu'ayyed and Manṣūr, and the Amīrs who were in Egypt to make preparations and to set forth on the expedition, any man who did not go was to send a substitute. It was said that some of the executive officials, servants, and eunuchs were charged to provide a considerable sum of money to help the Sulṭān. He at once set about the sale of clothing, arms, provisions, woollen stuffs, furs, sables, Ba'lbec coats, and other things. He also took some money from the Sulṭān al-Ghūrī's son with which to provide pay.

It was reported that the Sulṭān sent some of the court officials to Atābek Ḳīt al-Raḥbī to escort him from the fortress of Alexandria to that of Damietta. He also sent imperial instructions to Ẓāhir Ḳānṣūh, at the fortress of Alexandria, that he was to reside in the palace of al-Malik al-Mu'ayyed at Alexandria, that he was to ride to the mosque, and celebrate the Friday prayers with the people, and to make excursions in the direction of the gardens of Alexandria.

On Friday, the 25th, Amīr Khāir Bey, Architect, one of the chief Amīrs, with Amīr Ezbek, the Gunner, left for the expedition with the usual military procession.

On Saturday, the 26th, the troops went up for an inspection parade, but none of the chief Amīrs paraded, and the Sulṭān concealed himself in Dahīshah ; so the troops returned to their homes after a fruitless errand.

On the same day the Sulṭān issued a proclamation forbidding all excesses by the people, and that no Jew or Christian was to sell wine, beer, or hashīsh, under penalty of being hanged forthwith. But no one paid any attention to this order, and things went on just as before.

On Thursday, the 1st, the newly appointed judges of the previous month went to congratulate the Sulṭān on the new month, and then returned to their homes. The Sulṭān then informed the troops that pay would be issued on Saturday, the 3rd. He had agreed to pay fifty dīnārs to each Memlook, and also five months arrears of meat rations and forage allowance, which gave them satisfaction. The Sulṭān also appointed about ten members of the Court to be Amīrs of Tens, amongst them one named Khāir Bey al-Bajmakdār, one of the best Memlooks of Ashraf Ḳāit Bai. He also, it was said, distributed one thousand dīnārs amongst the dervishes in the monasteries and shrines at Ḳarāfah and elsewhere. He further gave five ardebbs of wheat to each monastery, desiring them to pray for victory to the Sulṭān and destruction to the enemy. He also caused to be read a number of khatmahs from the Ḳor'ān at the shrines, including those of the Imām al-Shāfi'ī, the Imām al-Laith, and others.

The Sulṭān also urged the descendants of the Sulṭāns, the Amīrs, and executive officials to make early payment of the sums assigned them towards the pay of the troops. It was said that he took a considerable sum of money from the Sulṭān al-Ghūrī's son, and that al-Ghūrī had, before he left for Syria, assigned to his son the amount of one hundred thousand dīnārs; such at least was the report.

On Saturday, the 3rd, the troops went up to the citadel to receive their pay, in compliance with the Sulṭān's orders. [86] On that same day came the bad news that the army that had gone to Gaza had suffered defeat on Sunday, the 24th, of Dhu'l Ka'dah. Strangely enough, al-Ghūrī's previous defeat took place on Sunday, the 25th of Rejeb, there being only a difference of one day in the two dates, a remarkable coincidence.

Briefly the account was as follows: Jān Birdī al-Ghazālī started for the expedition a few days in advance of the troops, the latter and the Amīrs following in batches in a very dilatory manner. Seeing their delay in joining, al-Ghazālī collected a party of Arabs and, accompanied by Amīr Erzamak al-Nāshif, one of the chief Amīrs, who had been appointed Governor of Ḥamāh, and Dōlāt Bai, Governor of Gaza, originally one of al-Ghūrī's Memlooks, with a body of the Sultan's Memlooks advanced to Gaza. Marching along the Sulṭān's road, they cut across Ibn 'Othmān's force, and a fierce battle ensued at al-Sherī'at near Baisān. The Ottoman troops were commanded by Sinān Pasha, who had Amīrs and a large body of Turkish troops under him. The force with Jān Birdī was only a small one. A most terrible fight ensued between them, enough to turn one's hair grey. It resulted in the defeat of Jān Birdī and his Amīrs and troops. Many Amīrs were amongst the slain. [Names omitted.]

* * * * *

Amīr Jān Birdī al-Ghazālī and Amīr Erzamak al-Nāshif were reported wounded, a great number of the Royal Memlooks and servants were killed and their heads hacked about with swords.

This news was said to have come from al-Amīr Ṭakṭ Bai, High Chamberlain. It was just after he had left to take part in the expedition, and was waiting at Ṣāliḥiyyeh, that some of the Royal Memlooks came and reported what had happened. So he sent to tell the Sulṭān of the terrible conflict. It was said that Ibn 'Othmān's men had taken possession of the baggage of al-Ghazālī and Erzamak al-Nāshif, after the battle, and that they were left with neither baggage nor arms, nor horses nor camels. This second victory added fresh vigour to the Ottoman troops. Of the Egyptians, only he escaped whose life was destined to be prolonged. It was said that al-Ghūrī's Memlooks were those who had noticed the army (of the Turks), and were the first to flee, and so brought about this second defeat.

In view of the many different reports, Amīr Sunbul, chief

of the Memlooks, was sent to Ṣāliḥiyyeh to obtain intelligence, and he started at once.

On Sunday, the 4th, this terrible incident occurred: The Sulṭān went to the Maidān and was joined by the Amīrs and troops. Suddenly a great clamour arose in Rumailah, and the report was spread that Ibn 'Othmān's army had arrived at Raidāniyyeh. Then the Sulṭān said: "How many times have you been ordered to march off on the expedition, and have been unwilling to go; go out now and meet Ibn 'Othmān!" So the troops armed themselves and marched off; and there was a horrible clamour in Cairo, and people stored away their clothing in secret places. In the midst of all this confusion, [87] the troops mounted and proceeded to Raidāniyyeh, but finding that the Turks were not there, they returned to their homes, after Cairo had been convulsed and people had made up their minds to hide in the cemeteries. It then appeared that a party of Arabs had come down from the hills to Raidāniyyeh, and a man who saw them at a distance reported that they were Turks, and this false report was published in Cairo. To-day the Sulṭān released Amīr Ḳānṣūh al-Ashrafī, formerly Governor of Aleppo, who had surrendered the citadel without resistance (p. 73).

* * * * *

On Monday, the 5th, the remnant of the Amīrs and troops who had been defeated at Gaza by Ibn 'Othmān returned to Cairo. Among them was Jān Birdī al-Ghazālī and Erzamak al-Nāshif, and certain subordinate Amīrs. They arrived in the most pitiable state, the plunder and slaughter had been worse than before. Some of the imperial Memlooks came back on donkeys, some on camels, all having been deprived of uniforms, horses, and arms.

None survived, in fact, but a few for whom fate had so decreed. They said that some of Ibn 'Othmān's troops were armed with hooks on their lances, with which they dragged the rider from his horse, and threw him on the ground. Jān Birdī said that he was thus thrown down, and had it not been for his servants who defended him from the Turks, they would have hacked his head, as they did that of Amīr Khūdā Birdī, who was killed.

They also said that Ibn 'Othmān's troops were in numbers as swarms of locusts; that some of them were armed with muskets (firing a leaden bullet), and were carried in wooden carts, drawn by oxen and buffaloes, moving at the head of the advanced guard; and many other things of this nature.

Amongst those who also returned were Amīr Dolāt Bai, Governor of Gaza, and there at the time of the battle; Amīr Bakhsh Bai, Inspector of Granaries, brother of Amīr Kurt Bai, formerly Vālī of Cairo, wrongly reported as killed in the battle of Merj Dābek; he had been hiding with the Arabs. There also returned one of the subordinate Amīrs, Ḳirḳmās al-Raḥbī, reported killed in the same battle, and many others.

On the arrival of Jān Birdī al-Ghazālī and Amīr Erzamak al-Nāshif at the citadel, the Sulṭān clothed them in sleeveless robes, lined with ermine, and they returned to their homes. There was general rejoicing at their safety for they were Knights of Islām, and bands played in their honour outside their houses.

On the return of al-Ghazalī with the Amīrs and troops, the correct list of losses was ascertained, and in every quarter there was mourning, as if it were the Days of Judgment.

Orders were given by the Sulṭān that the first issue of pay would be on Tuesday, the 6th. Early on the morning of this day the troops went up to the citadel, and the Sulṭān began to pay them, giving each Memlook twenty-five dīnārs, including the usual money for the feast of "Sacrifices". He had first offered them thirty dīnārs each, and this they had refused; but when they saw how serious matters were, and [88] that Ibn 'Othmān was advancing and had even reached Ḳatīyā, they agreed to accept twenty-five dīnārs. They went down from the citadel and set about arming themselves for departure.

The same day the Sulṭān received the bad news that

Sinān Pasha, one of Ibn 'Othmān's Amīrs, who had taken possession of the town of Gaza, had put the people of the place to the sword, killing about a thousand—men, women, and children.

This act was perpetrated for the following reason :—

During the engagement between al-Ghazālī and Sinān Pasha, a report was spread in Gaza that al-Ghazālī had gained a victory over the troops of Ibn 'Othmān, and had killed Sinān Pasha, whereupon 'Alī Bai, Deputy Dawādār of Gaza, and his troops set to work to plunder the Turkish camp, burning their tents and killing those Turks who were in camp and in the town, about 400, including old men, children, and the sick. As soon as the battle had gone against the Egyptian troops and their Amīrs, Sinān Pasha returned to Gaza, where he discovered the destruction that had been wrought. He then assembled all the people of Gaza, and asked them who had committed such outrages ; they replied, " 'Alī Bai, the Dawādār of the Deputy of Gaza, and his soldiers ; we did none of it." Sinān Pasha then ordered a surprise search to be made in the houses of Gaza ; uniform and horses were found in them belonging to the Turks. Then Sinān Pasha said, " When we entered Gaza did we disturb any of you, or plunder you of anything ? " They replied, " No." He said, " Why have you done so to our troops ? " to which they had no answer or excuse to make. Then he ordered his soldiers to put them to the sword, and they massacred a multitude of them ; good and bad perished together. Such was the divine decree, and it has been rightly said, " If Fate brings thee into distress through the sins of thy past life, ask God to remove it, for He alone can do so."

On Wednesday, the 7th, a number of nomad tribesmen of Ghazālah, Muḥārib, and Huwārāh, arrived at the royal gates. The Sulṭān had compelled the Arab Sheikhs to bring a number of their bravest Arab horsemen to accompany his troops on the expedition. The Arabs assembled in great numbers at Gizeh, and went thence to the Rūmailah to parade before the

Sulṭān in the Maidān. The prestige of the Memlooks had been damaged in the eyes of the Arabs and Fellāḥīn on account of the defeats suffered at the hands of the Turks. Ibn 'Othmān was in possession of Syria, the people felt sure that the Circassian Dynasty was tottering, and that it was Ibn 'Othmān who was master of the country. Some of the people in reply to a demand from their Sulṭān, said, "We cannot pay tribute until we are sure whether the country belongs to you or to Ibn 'Othmān ; we do not want to pay it twice over. In fact, confusion reigns on land and sea ; Heaven only knows what will happen."

On that day it was reported that the Sulṭān had given orders for the messenger, before mentioned, who came from Ibn 'Othmān, to be drowned; and it was said that he had been actually drowned by night, and the Turks who were with him.

At this time the Sulṭān began to distribute the grants to the troops for the Feast of Sacrifices, but he did not give any [89] to the Memlooks defeated with Ghazālī, saying, "You ran away and did not fight at all ; you betrayed the Amīrs, so that they suffered a defeat." At this time also a rumour ran amongst the people that the vanguard of Ibn 'Othmān's army had reached Ḳaṭīyā, and had taken the citadel of Ṭīnah, which had been destroyed by its inhabitants. This report, however, lacked confirmation.

Saturday, the 17th, was the Feast of Sacrifices, so the Sulṭān took part in the festival prayers, the Amīrs attending, as usual, in full-dress uniform. There was a grand festival procession, but the people were in great fear and trembling on account of Ibn 'Othmān . . . particularly on what they had heard of the plundering and killing of the people of Gaza, the taking captive of the women, and the massacre of the children.

On Monday, the 12th, the Sulṭān paraded the Royal ammunition column, which was to accompany the force. The wooden vehicles which he had made for the expedition were driven past him, as he was seated on the Maidān. There were a hundred in all (known by the Turks as 'Arabahs), each one being drawn by a pair of oxen. They carried brass guns which fired leaden balls.

The Sulṭān came down from his seat and mounted his charger, holding a baton in his hand, and attended to the proper arrangement of the vehicles as they went by. Then wagons followed and two hundred camels bearing about 1,500 large shields, also powder, lead, iron, and wooden lances, etc. In front of the wagons were four drums and fifes; in front of all marched some two hundred sharpshooters, consisting of Turcomans and Maghribis carrying white Ba'lbec standards, saying, "God make the Sulṭān victorious." They were also accompanied by a body of slaves and others, bearing naphtha to throw in front of the wagons. At the head of the column rode Amīr Moghul Bai, the Chief Armourer, and Yūsuf, Second Armourer, a number of the armoury rank and file, and 'Abd al-Bāsiṭ, Superintendent. Al-Shihābī Aḥmed Ibn Ṭūlūnī went with them, and a great number of carpenters and blacksmiths, who had been detailed for the expedition.

They went out into the Rumailah by the Maidān gate, passing by the tombs and on through Bastīyīn by the Zawīlah-gate, and Cairo city. The streets resounded as they went through, and the people lined their shops to see the sight. It was a memorable day, and the people prayed for victory over Ibn 'Othmān, the rebel. They wept when they beheld these wagons and guns, and realized the great enterprise of the Sulṭān. The column continued its way through Cairo, and emerging at the Bāb al-Naṣr, proceeded to Raidāniyyeh, halting near the tomb of al-'Ādil there. It was reported that a woman was crushed to death in the crowd. On the arrival of the wagons at the tomb of al-'Ādil they were drawn up there to await the Amīrs; it was a day to be remembered as a spectacle.

On Tuesday, the 13th, some people interceded for the Memlooks from Gaza, who had not received the grant for the

Feast of Sacrifices from the Sulṭān. So the latter paid them that day, after reprimanding them again, saying, [90] "You fled and brought a defeat on the Amīrs; you did not fight at all, and disgraced yourselves in the eyes of the people."

On Wednesday, the 14th, al-Nāsirī Muḥammed Ibn Shems al-Dīn al-Kūsūnī, the Chief Doctor arrived at the Palace. He had been a prisoner of Ibn 'Othmān's in Aleppo, and escaped thence with the Arabs, and for a considerable sum of money they brought him to Egypt. He went up and had an audience of the Sulṭān. He had altered his appearance, shaved his chin, and disguised himself as an Arab, and thus managed to escape. He told his story to the Sulṭān, and said that Ibn 'Othmān's troops were mutinous; that he had lost an enormous number of camels and horses owing to snow in Syria; that the prices of everything were exorbitant; that the troops were suffering from the cold and the snow, and the loss of their horses. It was reported that Ibn 'Othmān's troops had been in Gaza and had left it and were fleeing to the hills; and that the Arabs were killing many of those whom they found in the villages. On Thursday, the 15th, the soldiers went up to receive their pay, but the eunuchs said to them: "Sirs, there is no pay to-day; the country is laid waste, the roads are infested by the Arabs, and the collectors and the Sheikhs of the Arabs have not sent any of the amounts due from them. If by Monday any of it is received it shall be paid to you." So the troops left the citadel distressed. It was six months since they had received an issue of ration-meat, and their pay was in arrears as well.

The same day the Sulṭān conferred a robe of honour on Ḳānṣūh Rajlah, one of the chief Amīrs, who had been Governor of Ḳaṭīyā, and appointed him Inspector of the Sharḳīeh Provinces instead of Ḳajmās, who had been found incapable of improving their condition. Elmās, the Western Inspector, retained his post; and Amīr Abrak, the Vizīr and Ustādār, also retained his; the latter's dismissal had been reported.

Egyptian affairs had then fallen into great confusion owing to a variety of causes.

On Friday the Sulṭān took part in the prayers of the day. Then he conferred a distinction on Atābek Sūdūn al-Dawādārī, and appointed him to command the troops on the expedition. At this time, also, Amīr Ṭakṭ Bai, the Chief Chamberlain, arrived. He had started with the expedition to Gaza, but had declared himself ill and remained at Ṣāliḥiyyeh. After the defeat of Jān Birdī al-Ghazālī, and his return to Egypt, the rest of the Amīrs remained at Ṣāliḥiyyeh waiting for the departure of the second expedition. So when Amir Ṭakṭ Bai arrived without the others, the Amīrs were distressed. The Amīrs and the troops considered him incapable; in fact, he was detested by the whole army. On this day the Sulṭān ordered the Arab tribesmen who had arrived in the city to return to their homes, as the Amīrs had pointed out to him that the Arabs would be of no use on the expedition.

During this month the Sulṭān conferred a distinction on [91] Amīr Īnāl, treasurer to al-Amīr Ṭarā Bai, one of the Amīrs of Tens, and appointed him Governor of Damietta, instead of the existing governor.

On Sunday, the 18th, the Sulṭān received the bad news that Ibn ʻOthmān himself had left Syria with his army, and was marching on Egypt. He was said to have divided his forces into two, and to be sending one army along the royal route and another through the desert.

On receipt of this news the Sulṭān assembled the Amīrs, and a council of war was held. It was reported that he would himself go to Raidāniyyeh and remain there, and that the troops would be formed into two forces, one going in the direction of ʻAjrūd and the other to the place whence the messenger had come. The Amīrs had decided that the expedition should be dispatched at the beginning of the new year; but when this bad news reached them confusion reigned among them, and the Sulṭān ordered them to send out tents quickly to Raidāniyyeh, and to be on the look-out, as Ibn 'Othmān had reached Gaza.

It was said that he had gone to visit Jerusalem, and would then march with his troops into Egypt. Some said one thing and some another, so that people were at a loss where to go till this trouble should be over. The Sulṭān ordered the Inspector of the troops to go round to all the Amīrs to urge them to send their tents to Raidāniyyeh that day—so this was done.

The Sulṭān also issued a proclamation to all Maghribis in Egypt and Cairo to parade for inspection the next day.

On Monday, the 19th, the Sulṭān took his seat on the dais in the courtyard, and a great number of the Maghribis came up, but on their arrival at the citadel the Sulṭān did not go out to meet them; he sent Amīr Shād Bey, the "one-eyed", to them, who said: "The Sultan commands you to select a thousand of your bravest men to take part in the expedition." Whereupon they sent to the Sulṭān, saying: "It is not our custom to go with the army; we are only to fight against the Franks, and not against Muḥammedans," and they showed they were on Ibn 'Othmān's side.

The Sulṭān was annoyed by their reply, and sent to tell them that if they did not go out to fight the imported Memlooks would kill all the Maghribis in Egypt to the last man.

At this time it was reported that Ibn 'Othmān had sent a letter to the Sheikh of the Arabs, Aḥmed Ibn Baḳar, offering him a pardon, saying: "Enter into our allegiance and receive our pardon, and meet us at Ṣāliḥiyyeh with a thousand ardebbs of barley." It was said that 'Abd al-Dā'im Aḥmed Ibn Baḳar, who was a rebel, had gone to Ibn 'Othmān to Gaza, and there were endless stories in circulation about Ibn 'Othmān.

On this Monday also the Sulṭān ordered a parade of all ranks for the following day at Raidāniyyeh, fully accoutred. The Sulṭān went down to the Maidān, said the afternoon prayers, then rode off to Raidāniyyeh and remained in camp there, for the first time since his accession.

On Tuesday, the 20th, the troops paraded under arms for inspection of the Sulṭān. That day the chief Amīrs went out to Raidāniyyeh, that is, the Amīrs detailed for the expedition. They went out in detachments fully armed (? ? ?). [92] Ṭaḳṭ Bai, Chief Chamberlain, was said to be excused for ill-health, but most probably he went. The rest of the chief Amīrs of thousands started off, all the Amīrs of Ṭablkhānāh and Tens, and the Egyptian troops; only a small number of Amīrs and soldiers remained behind.

There were more troops employed on this expedition than under al-Ghūrī, and this Sulṭān had displayed great energy in making wagons and forging guns, in the manufacture of muskets, and the raising of a very large number of musketeers. In all this he showed a great amount of energy and high purpose, hoping that Allah would give him the victory over Ibn 'Othmān, for the latter had attacked the Egyptian army without provocation, and for every tyrant there exists somewhere a place or mode of death.

The Sulṭān gave orders that when they fought in three days' time the big elephants should accompany the troops into battle. On their departure that day the Sulṭān rode from his camp to the Maṣṭabah at Raidāniyyeh, the place where the rations were served out. He sat there while a great concourse of men assembled under arms, covering the whole plain. There also were gathered the great majority of the common people, and even the women; shouts were raised and prayers uttered for victory for the Sulṭān. It was a memorable day, and when the Sulṭān looked at the troops he did not inspect them there, but proclaimed that the troops of all ranks were to assemble at Ṣāliḥiyyeh for inspection, and that he would not go there until after the troops were assembled, and that he would then return to the citadel; the latter was the proper course to take.

On Thursday, the 24th, the Sulṭān was still at Raidāniyyeh, and on that day the remnant of the troops left. There was no excuse for their departure being prolonged, the Sulṭān having urged them to start with the utmost dispatch.

When the Sulṭān left the citadel he took with him Ḳāsim Bey, one of Ibn 'Othmān's sons, the boy of whom mention has been made. The Sulṭān had given him a special outfit and ornaments, and ordered him to go with the troops, and to stand, when in action, under the Royal Standard. It was said that Ibn 'Othmān was uneasy about this boy, and that the majority of his soldiers were favourably inclined towards him, and said that if Selīm Shāh were defeated they had no one but their master's son to succeed him.

The same day there was a report that the Ruler of Rhodes had sent the Sulṭān a thousand musketeers, and a number of ships containing powder ; that these ships had entered the port of Damietta ; and that they were sent by the Ruler of Rhodes to help the Sulṭān of Egypt against Ibn 'Othmān, who had designs upon Egypt. But nothing came of this ; it was mere idle rumour without foundation.

When the Sulṭān went out to Raidāniyyeh it was said that he would proceed to Ṣāliḥiyyeh to meet Ibn 'Othmān's
[93] forces, but the Amīrs prevented his going, telling him that fighting would only take place between them at Raidāniyyeh.

The merchants began to transfer their goods from the shops in the market into secret places for safe keeping, but none of their goods escaped. On that day most people removed from the suburbs and went into Cairo, and lived there.

The well-to-do people moved their belongings to the monasteries, schools, and burial-grounds, and to the houses of the common folk in the grazing grounds for safe keeping ; but none of their property escaped, as will be seen later.

At the end of this year Shihābī Aḥmed Ibn al-Amīr Asnbaghā al-Ṭayyārī died ; he was formerly Chief of the Guards, and belonged to a family of chiefs. He was a venerable and excellent chief ; he was nearly 90 when he died, and one of the oldest inhabitants of the land.

On Thursday, the 22nd, news came that Ibn 'Othmān

had left Gaza, and that his advanced guard had reached 'Arīsh. It was reported that the Sulṭān had ordered a trench to be dug from the fountain of 'Allān up to Jebel Aḥmer (red mountain) and beyond the fields of Maṭariyyeh, and he then erected large shields along that trench, the guns were drawn up and arranged round them and the wooden carriages, already mentioned as having been made at the citadel. Then the Sulṭān ordered Amīr Māmāy al-Ṣaghīr, the Inspector of Markets, to issue a proclamation to the shop-keepers, chandlers, bakers, and butchers in Cairo to bring their goods to the camp at the tomb of al-'Ādil, and establish a market there for the troops. The Sulṭān instructed the Vālī to proclaim that all the soldiers who had remained behind should go out to Raidāniyyeh. So the torch-bearers (?) gave it out in the quarters and streets that the Royal Memlooks were to go out to the camp that day, under penalty of being hung forthwith at their own doors. The Sulṭān caused this to be proclaimed twice on that day, for he learnt that many of the Royal Memlooks used to go out early in the morning to the camp, so that the Sulṭān might see them, and return to spend the night in their houses, and this displeased the Sulṭān, and he ordered them to spend every night in camp.

On Friday, the 23rd, news came that Ibn 'Othman's advance guard had reached Ḳaṭīyā, which greatly disturbed the people. On Saturday, the 24th, the Sulṭān inspected the troops in camp, and the whole body of them paraded. The Sulṭān promised them that if they fought bravely against Ibn 'Othmān's army and defeated them he would pay them ten ashrafīs each, and give each of them a sword and shield. He ordered Amīr Ans Bai, Master of the Horse, to effect a reconciliation between the roughs of al-Ṣalībah and the roughs of the town. It was reported on that day that the Sulṭān set to work to construct a wall to protect the guns which he had posted at Raidāniyyeh, and that the Sulṭān carried some of the stones himself with the workmen. When the soldiers saw that the Sulṭān was carrying stones himself the Memlooks set to work to do the same, and to help the workmen to excavate the ditch and make the wall for the protection of the guns.

Then the news arrived that Ibn 'Othmān's troops had [94] reached Belbeis.

On Sunday, the 25th, al-Amīr Ḳānṣūh al-'Adilī, the Inspector of the Sharḳīeh, returned. The Sulṭān had sent him to find out information about Ibn 'Othmān's forces when they had arrived near Ṣāliḥiyyeh. When the Amīr Ḳānṣūh reached Ṣāliḥiyyeh he saw that a party of Ibn 'Othman's men were there. He captured two of them, decapitated them, and brought their heads before the Sulṭān. With them was a man from Aleppo, belonging to Khāir Bey, the Governor, who had intrigued against the Sulṭān al-Ghūrī and joined Ibn 'Othmān. This man gave the following information to the Sulṭān, Ṭūmān Bai:—

"Khāir Bey, Governor of Aleppo, is coming against you with Ibn Suwār and a number of Ibn 'Othmān's Amīrs and an advanced guard of 8,000 of his cavalry. But their horses are exhausted with fatigue and hunger, and food is scarce among the troops." On this man were found a number of letters from Khāir Bey, Governor of Aleppo, to the chief Amīrs in Egypt. So the Sulṭān took the letters and put the man in irons.

It was reported that the commander of Ibn 'Othmān's force, on entering into Belbeis, proclaimed pardon and security, promising that none of the inhabitants, nor the fellāḥīn, should be ill-treated by the Turkish soldiers. Next came the news that Ibn 'Othmān's troops were at 'Ikrishah.

On learning this the Sulṭān was anxious to go out with the troops and engage them then and there, but he was prevented by the Amīrs. It would have been for the best had he done so, as their horses were at a standstill from fatigue and hunger, and most of Ibn 'Othmān's force had marched on foot from the time they left Syria and were extremely tired. The Sulṭān would probably have been able to defeat them before they could reach Khānkāh and find supplies of fodder and drink and could rest from their fatigues. But the Amīrs would not have it so, and the Turks succeeded in entering Khānkāh. Then the Sulṭān ordered his troops to pass that night in front of the camp in the saddle, fully accoutred, and only to sleep in turns for fear of a night attack. An intense fear of Ibn 'Othmān's forces now prevailed amongst the Circassians. On the approach of his army to Khānkāh most of the inhabitants left with their families and goods, and went into Cairo for fear of plunder and massacre by the Turks. Then the Sālimī Arabs began to lay hold of any Turks they could catch, and, decapitating them, brought their heads to the Sulṭān, who ordered them to be hung up on the Bāb al-Naṣr, and Bab Zawīlah.

The Sulṭān inspected the troops in Raidāniyyeh, fully accoutred, with the chief and subordinate Amīrs; the former were accompanied by the drums and fifes, and it was an important day. The Sulṭān then went out to Birkah al-Hāj [95] with the Amirs and all the troops; he returned to camp preceded by torches, drums, and fifes.

The columns of troops extended from Jebel al-Aḥmer to the fields of Maṭariyyeh, the whole plain was covered with them. It was said that the Sulṭān, on hearing that Ibn 'Othmān was at Belbeis, ordered that the granaries there and in the neighbourhood, and even those in Khānkāh, should be burnt. Great quantities of straw, bran, wheat, barley, and beans were burnt, to save them from Ibn 'Othmān's troops, who required them for themselves and their horses, and would have been thus strengthened for the fight.

The following incident was said to have happened before the end of this year. The Sulṭān was sitting in his tent when a Turcoman entered wearing a red cap and a quiver, with a muffler drawn over his face. The Sulṭān had a few of his suite with him. On approaching the Sulṭān he was pushed back by some of the eunuchs, who were standing by, and when his chest was touched a pair of long breasts were found, and the blanket being drawn off a Turcoman woman was revealed. The Sulṭān, suspecting she had come to murder him, ordered her to be taken out. They then found that the woman was wearing a coat of mail under her clothes, and was carrying a large dagger. The imported Memlooks, seeing this, struck at her with their swords. They felt sure she had meant to murder the Sultan. After she had been killed the Sulṭān ordered her to be suspended on the Bāb al-Naṣr.

Then the Sulṭān sent two heads by the Vālī's Dawādār; one was thought to be that of Ibrāhīm al-Samarḳandī, and the other that of one of Ibn 'Othmān's Amīrs. Both were fastened up over a shop by the Zawīlah-gate.

One of the Arabs had plotted against Ibrāhīm Samarḳandi; he had entertained him, and Samarḳandi spent the night with him; he had come with Ibn 'Othmān's forces. During the night the Bedouin cut his head off, and at daybreak took it to the Sulṭān, Ṭūmān Bai, and asked him what he would give to the person who would bring him Ibrāhīm Samarḳandī's head. The Sulṭān said: "A thousand dīnārs." He then produced the head from under his cloak, saying, "Here it is." After having this verified, the Sulṭān paid him the thousand dīnārs.

Ibrāhīm Samarkandī came originally from al-Medīnah. He travelled from Persia to Turkey, and was acquainted with the Turkish language. He went into Egypt and became one of the Sulṭān's al-Ghūrī' personal friends. On the latter's defeat he joined Selīm Shāh Ibn 'Othmān, and became one of his suite. It was said that it was he who suggested to Ibn 'Othmān that he should enter Egypt and take possession of it [96] and exterminate the Circassians. Samarḳandī was a great tyrant, and had he lived to see Ibn 'Othmān in possession of Egypt the people would never have received any good from him, and he himself brought all sorts of charges against the dignitaries of Egypt. But Allah gave the people relief from his evil ways.

On Wednesday, the 28th, news arrived that Ibn 'Othmān's

advanced guard was at Birkah al-Ḥāj, which put the military in Cairo into a state of great consternation. They closed the Bāb al-Futūḥ and Bāb al-Naṣr, and the Bāb al-Sha'riyyeh, also the Bāb al-Baḥr and the Bāb al-Kanṭarah, and other gates of the town. The markets in Cairo were closed, the mills were stopped, and bread and flour became scarce.

As soon as the Sulṭān had confirmation of the reports that Ibn 'Othmān's army had arrived at Birkah al-Ḥāj, he sounded the alarm in camp. All the troops and chief Amīrs and the Amīrs of Ṭablkhānāh and of Tens, and Kāsim Bey Ibn 'Othmān mounted. The total of the assembled forces, including the Royal Memlooks and Arabs, amounted to some 20,000 horsemen, with about thirty standards. The drums and fifes sounded to battle, and the Sulṭān Ṭūmān Bai rode round, personally posted the Amīrs according to their ranks, and drew up his forces from Jebel Aḥmer to the fields of Maṭariyyeh. An immense force was assembled, and the Sulṭān displayed a lofty courage(?). Had the Sulṭān al-Ghūrī been alive he would not have done a fraction of what Sulṭān Ṭūmān Bai did. But Allah did not grant him the victory over Ibn 'Othmān. No battle took place that day between the opposing forces, neither of them went out to meet the adversary. On that day a few Turks' heads were cut off and sent to be suspended on the gates of the city.

On Thursday, the 29th, a tremendous engagement took place, the mere mention of which is enough to strike terror into the hearts of men and its horrors to unhinge their reason.

To sum up, it may be said that the Sulṭān Ṭūmān Bai, after encamping at Raidāniyyeh, fortified it with cannons and guns, arranged a line of shields and wooden defences for them, and dug a trench from Jebel Aḥmer to the Maṭariyyeh fields. In rear of the guns he placed about a thousand camel loads of sacks of forage, and on the pack-saddles he fastened white and red banners, which fluttered in the breeze. He also collected a number of oxen to draw the vehicles. He expected a long battle between himself and Ibn 'Othmān, or even a long siege; matters, however, turned out differently. Ibn 'Othmān's forces halted two days at Birkah al-Ḥāj, but the Sulṭān Ṭūmān Bai did not venture to advance against them; he ought to have done so, and given them battle there, before they could get into Raidāniyyeh. On Thursday Ibn 'Othmān's force came on, and his advanced guard reached Jebel Aḥmer. .

On learning this the Sulṭān sounded the alarm in camp, and ordered the troops to move out to engage Ibn 'Othmān's army. The drums beat to battle, the chief Amīrs and the whole force mounted, and extended across the plain. [97] Ibn 'Othmān's soldiers came on like locusts in multitude and they were superior in point of numbers. The two armies met in the outskirts of Raidāniyyeh, and a terrible battle ensued, which it would take long to describe, a greater battle than that which took place in Merj Dābeḳ. Countless numbers of the Turks were killed, including Sinān Pasha, Ibn 'Othman's former tutor and his Chief Vizīr, and a great many of his Amīrs. Their bodies lay scattered from 'Allān's fountain (?) to the tomb of Amīr Yeshbek, the Dawādār. Then the Turks recovered, coming up from every direction like clouds. They divided into two forces, one advancing under Jebel Aḥmer, and the other by the camp at Raidāniyyeh. The noise of their musketry was deafening, and their attack furious. In a short time countless numbers of Egyptian troops had fallen, including a great many of the chief Amīrs, among whom was Ezbek, the Gunner. Atābek Sūdūn, the Dawādār, was seriously wounded, some say that his thigh was broken and that he hid in a field there. Amīr 'Allān, the Dawādār, was also wounded. In the short space of about sixty minutes the Egyptian army was defeated and in full retreat.

Ṭūmān Bai stood his ground about eighty minutes after this, and fought on with a few of his armed slaves and Memlooks, inflicting great losses on Ibn 'Othmān's men. Finally, when the Turks were too many for him, finding himself deserted by his troops, and fearing capture, he folded up the Royal Standard, and ran and concealed himself; some say that he went towards Ṭarā.

This was the third defeat the Egyptian army had suffered. The Turkish force that had advanced under cover of Jebel Aḥmer, came down upon the tents of the Sulṭān, plundering everything, kit, arms, horses, camels, and oxen, including the guns the Sulṭān had put into position there, with the shields and palisading, and the vehicles on which the Sulṭān had spent so much time, labour, and money, and from which he had reaped no advantage. Everything in the camp was plundered. Such was the decree of Fate.

After the flight of the Sulṭān and the looting of the camp, numbers of Turks carried sword and violence into Cairo. Some proceeded to Maḳsharah, and burning the doors let out the prisoners, including a number of Turks whom the Sulṭān had imprisoned when he was at Raidāniyyeh. They also released all those in Dīlem and Raḥbah.

Then they went on to the house of Amīr Khāir Bey, the architect, one of the chief Amīrs, and plundered that. The house of Yūnus, the Interpreter, and those of many of the Amīrs, the leading executive officials, and people holding honourable positions were similarly treated. Rascals and slaves set to work to rob the houses under the mask of Turks, and firebrands were, as it were, thrown about amongst the people of the city. Many Turks entered the mills and took away the mules and worn-out horses and a number of camels belonging to the water-carriers. They plundered, in fact, everything [98] that came in their way, whether dry goods or anything else. The pillaging went on all that day until after sunset.

Then they went to the granaries in Cairo and Būlāk, and plundered the grain which was public property. No one had thought that they would do this, but such was the decree of Fate.

Ibn Suwār was killed at Raidāniyyeh in this engagement, and was buried in his grandfather's tomb, opposite the tomb of the Dawādār Yeshbek.

Sinān Pasha, Ibn 'Othmān's Vizīr, was also killed. Sheikh Bedr al-Dīn al-Zeitūnī wrote this lament :—

> " We weep over Egypt and her people—
> Her prosperous places have become desolate, and
> The once glorious has become the inglorious ! "

On Monday, the last week of the year A.H. 922, the Amīr of the Faithful, Mohammed al-Mutewekkil 'alā Allāh, entered Cairo, accompanied by Ibn 'Othmān's ministers, and a large force of Turkish soldiers. The following also returned :—

(1) Malik al-'Umarā Khāir Bey.
(2) Kemāl al-Dīn al-Ṭawīl, Chief Ḳāḍī of the Shāfi'ī Sect.
(3) The Māliki Ḳāḍī Muḥyī al-Dīn al-Demīrī.
(4) The Ḥanbalī Ḳāḍī Shihāb al-Dīn al-Futūḥī.

All these had been prisoners of Ibn 'Othmān since the death of the Sulṭān al-Ghūrī.

The Khalīfah entered by the Bāb al-Naṣr, and traversed Cairo, preceded by torch-bearers. He announced a public pardon, and general security and continuance of trade. No one was to be molested by the Turkish soldiers. It was further proclaimed that the door of oppression was closed and that of justice opened, and that whoever was found harbouring a Circassian Memlook would be hung forthwith.

The cry " Long live the victorious King Selīm Shāh ! " was raised on all sides.

These proclamations were, however, disregarded by the Turks, who fell to plundering people's houses and even the suburban villas under the pretext of searching for Circassian Memlooks. This pillaging and attacking the houses of the Amīrs, soldiers, and people continued for three days. Not a horse nor mule, nor clothing, nor anything great or small was left untouched.

About that time Yūnus al-'Ādilī returned, and Khushḳadam, who had been Inspector of Granaries in Egypt and had fled from al-Ghūrī to the Turkish dominions, and had instigated this great rebellion.

On Friday the Khuṭbah was delivered in the name of Sulṭān Selīm Shāh from the pulpits in Egypt and Cairo. Some of the preachers in their addresses referred to him as follows: "God save the Sulṭān, Ibn al-Sulṭān, King of the two continents and the two seas; conqueror of the two armies, Sulṭān of the two 'Irāks, servant of the two sacred cities, the victorious King Selīm Shāh. O Lord of both worlds, grant that he may ever be victorious."

This brings to a close our account of the events of the year A.H. 922.

The year ends with war and sorrow—the people are in the direst extremities. All this has come upon them in accordance with the decree of Fate.

[99] Then commenced the year A.H. 923, the first day of Muḥarrem being a Saturday.

To-day the Sulṭān Selīm Shāh sent a body of Janissaries and posted them at the gates of the city to prevent the houses being plundered. After the defeat of the Egyptian army the Sulṭān Selīm Shāh moved his camp from Birkah al-Ḥāj Raidāniyyeh. The Turks set to work to catch the Circassian Memlooks, taking them from the tombs and cemeteries and from the gardens of Maṭariyyeh, and bringing them before the Sulṭān, who ordered them to be decapitated.

Some Arab Sheiḳhs arrested Atābek Sūdūn Dawādārī and brought him before the Sulṭān Selīm Shāh. The latter abused him, and though he found that he was wounded and had a broken thigh, and was in a dying condition, he had no pity on him, but mounted him on a donkey, with a blue turban on his head, and publicly exposed him in his camp. He even intended to exhibit him in Cairo; but he died on the back of the donkey. It was said that they cut off his head after his death and hung it up in the camp. And so this slaughter of the Circassians continued; it was said that over four hundred Circassian slaves and Arabs from the Sharḳīeh and Gharbīeh provinces were slain.

Then Ibn 'Othmān sent for His Highness Muḥammed, son

of the Sulṭān al-Ghūrī, and dressed him in a green velvet and gold-embroidered ḳafṭān, and an 'Osmanli turban, and gave him a paper guaranteeing his safety, and issued instructions for him to reside in the college which his father had built at Sharābishīyīn.

Then Amīr Yūsuf al-Badrī, the Vizīr, went to the Sulṭān, received a pardon, was dressed in a velvet ḳāfṭān, and appointed Superintendent to the Gharbīeh provinces. The Sulṭān conferred robes of honour on :—

1. Amīr Fāris Seyfī Tamrāz, and appointed him Inspector of Minieh and other places in the North.

2. Al-Zeinī Berekāt Ibn Mūsā, and appointed him Inspector of Markets, empowering him to make what appointments he should think fit.

On Sunday, the 2nd, it was reported that the Ṣulṭān Selīm Shāh had moved his camp from Raidāniyyeh to Būlāḳ, where it occupied the ground from the embankment to the end of the central island, and that the keys of the citadel were brought there ; but he preferred to reside on the bank of the Nile.

As soon as a great many Turks had assembled in Cairo they began to reconnoitre the quarters, streets, and markets, and whenever they met people wearing red caps and small turbans they said to them, "You are Circassians," and beheaded them. So the people and even the Amīrs and royal princes took to wearing large turbans, and so the light turbans and caps were abolished in Egypt.

On Monday, the 3rd, the Sulṭān formed a cavalcade and entered Cairo by the Bāb al-Naṣr, and went through the city, preceded by an immense number of led horses and a large force of infantry and cavalry, which occupied the whole of the streets ; the procession went through the Zawīlah Gate under the Rab', and on to Būlāḳ, to the camp under the embankment. As the Sulṭān passed through the city he was cheered by all the populace.

He was described as having a fair complexion, a clean-shaven chin, and large nose and eyes, as being short in stature, and wearing a small turban. He showed levity and restlessness, turning his head from side to side as he rode along. He was said to be about forty years of age. He had not the dignity of former Sulṭāns. He was of an evil disposition, bloodthirsty, violent-tempered, and intolerant of being answered. As he passed through Cairo he was preceded by the Khalīfah, the four Judges, and a number of the executive officers. He issued proclamations daily in Cairo, assuring the public of security. Nevertheless, the plundering continued, his proclamations were ignored, and the people suffered extremely in consequence.

Amongst other things related of him was that he had given out at some of his councils in Damascus that on entering Egypt he would burn all the houses and put the people to the sword; but the Khalīfah was said to have induced him to give up that intention, otherwise there was nothing to prevent him carrying out his threat.

The damage inflicted by the Turks went on to such a degree that some of the upper classes and officials took to getting Turks to stand as guards at their doors, to prevent the spoiling of their houses. The Turks would arrest people in the streets, telling them they were Circassians; and when they declared that they were not, they would tell them to ransom themselves from death, and extort whatever sums of money they chose—so that the people really became their prisoners. The scum and the scoundrels of Egypt used to inform the 'Osmanlis of the resources of the princesses and ladies, and their costly clothing was carried off. In short, the treasure houses of the land fell into the hands of the Turks in Egypt, with clothing and weapons, horses, and mules, male and female slaves, and everything of value. They obtained there what they had never had in their own country, and what none of them had ever seen before, not even their great Master.

Stephen Austin & Sons, Ltd., Printers, Hertford.

www.ingramcontent.com/pod-product-compliance
Ingram Content Group UK Ltd.
Pitfield, Milton Keynes, MK11 3LW, UK
UKHW021408190726
13845UKWH00028B/946

9 789366 081588